Ellery H. Clark

Reminiscences of an Athlete

Salzwasser

Ellery H. Clark

Reminiscences of an Athlete

1. Auflage | ISBN: 978-3-84604-900-6

Erscheinungsort: Frankfurt, Deutschland

Erscheinungsjahr: 2020

Salzwasser Verlag GmbH

REMINISCENCES OF AN ATHLETE

REMINISCENCES OF AN ATHLETE

TWENTY YEARS ON TRACK AND FIELD

BY

ELLERY H. CLARK

All-around Athletic Champion of America, 1897, 1903
All-around Athletic Champion of New England,
1896, 1897, 1909, 1910

WITH ILLUSTRATIONS

BOSTON AND NEW YORK
HOUGHTON MIFFLIN COMPANY
The Riverside Press Cambridge
1911

CONTENTS

ILLUSTRATIONS

The illustrations at pages 10, 24, 40, 58, 88, 104, and 136 are from photographs by Hemment, N. Y.; the other illustrations are from photographs by The Pictorial News Co., N. Y.

REMINISCENCES OF AN ATHLETE

CHAPTER I

EARLY MEMORIES

I cannot remember the time when I was not interested in sport. There was no form of exercise which did not appeal to me, and this whether I took part myself, or, as a mere spectator, applauded the performance of others. To run fast or enduringly, to leap high or far, these had, for me, the savor of great deeds; and upon those who did them worthily, I gazed with awe, as upon beings of a superior world.

I am sure of the facts, yet when I look back and seek to find the reasons for them, I can scarcely seem to hit upon the cause. I was not reared in an athletic atmosphere; there were no family traditions to be maintained. It was, I think, simply a natural bent; the germ of the athletic fever was in my blood.

Stevenson has told us how he learned to write, not so much because he wished to be an author, although he wished that too, but principally, as it were, "in a wager with himself." And thus my own ambition, though a far less noble one, was in kind the same. I wished to be an athlete, yet it was not for the sake of the medals or the glory, although, to borrow Stevenson's phrase, perhaps "I wished that too." But my main incentive, like his, was a wager with myself. There was much that I aimed to acquire, yet it was not to excel others that I practised and trained. A certain standard of accomplishment was always before me; and to know, in my own heart, that I had attained it — that was my desire.

I had two playmates, in these early days, both inspired with the same ambition as myself. The result was a union of forces, and while all Boston knows that its athletic club, the B. A. A., was formed in 1887, how many Bostonians, I wonder, though skilled in local history, know that before this there was a B. A. C., which flourished in 1881, and a year or so later languished and died. Yet such was the fact, for my two friends and I were its founders. And although, as it seems to me now, scarce old enough to read and write, we had a constitution and by-laws. More than that, we had a club badge, a little oblong of crimson silk, with the letters B. A. C. embroidered upon it in gold, and a silver pin with which to fasten it to our coats. An air of mystery, dear to all small boys, surrounded us, and thus no profane outsider was ever to guess the existence of our Club. Except in secret meeting, the order of the letters was to be reversed, and to the ear of the world, we were to talk only of the doings of a certain "CAB." Altogether, we were quite elaborate, and existed, as I say, for upwards of a year.

Winter was the principal time for our diversions. We played football in the autumn, baseball in the spring, and devoted the time between to our Club. My parents lived in a tall house, opposite Boston Common, and half way down the slope of Beacon Hill. The house was deep and narrow, with long hallways connecting the rooms at either end; and the topmost story of all, away up under the big skylight, was our gymnasium, athletic field and running track, all in one. Here, as the fancy moved us, we practised our different sports — boxed and wrestled, jumped and ran. How the ceilings ever held is a mystery; and even more wonderful still seems the way in which my parents contrived to stand the noise. They endured it without complaint, and only once, that I recall, put a stop to any of our plans. That was in the days of the tug-of-war; not the good, old-fashioned kind where the contestants, a dozen or more on a side, pulled standing erect in the open, but a modern version of the game, where four men on each team lay prone upon the floor, feet braced against huge wooden cleats, and strained upon the rope until their faces purpled and the veins stood out upon their swollen necks. We had seen the Harvard teams in the Hemenway Gymnasium; and so, of course, must go forth and do likewise. Our hallway appeared to us an ideal place for the practice of the sport. We had everything planned — the purchase of the rope, the cleats, and all — and then my parents, consulting the family physician, promptly and very cruelly (as it seemed to us) vetoed our scheme, and the tug-of-war was never held.

Of all our varied pastimes, one stands out with special clearness in my mind. That was the running high jump. Later in our careers, we were to have a regular set of jumping standards, and a cross-bar as well; but when our club was founded, such luxuries were far beyond our means. And yet we did not lack inventiveness. Two chairs, placed on either side of the hall, were our standards, and a broom from the dusting closet served us as a bar. So far, so good; yet the problem of raising and lowering our broomstick still confronted us. To a certain extent, to be sure, we were aided by the natural construction of the chairs. The bar, supported on the lower rungs, formed the obstacle for the first jump; the higher rungs were next to be achieved; and if these were safely cleared, the broomstick was placed across the seats themselves. This last, indeed, was a dizzy height, to be approached with caution, with much shuffling of feet and grim contortion of face, after the manner of those real champions who were at once our envy and despair. Occasionally one of us, more, I think, by luck than skill, would clear it, but for the most part we would fail, with much damage to knees and shins; and thus, for a year or more, we were untroubled by the question of farther heights. Yet gradually, as we increased in strength and agility, the feat at which we had balked grew easier of accomplishment; the problem of raising the bar must be met and solved; and we turned, in our perplexity, to our "box of blocks," banished, for the moment, to the entry closet, as toys for children, having no place in an athlete's world.

I wonder if the modern boy gets all the fun that we did from such blocks of wood. Ours came, I remember, in an oblong cart. They were part brown, part white; and were intended, I suppose, solely for the construction of houses and castles of varying design. But our imagination was not thus to be circumscribed. It was not alone a double debt that the blocks contrived to pay, but one fifty or a hundred fold. Indians and settlers, redcoats and continentals, knights and paladins (I never felt sure, I think, just what a paladin really was, but the name echoed like music in my ears), ships and athletes, wild beasts and race-horses—Heaven alone knows what those humble blocks, at one time and another, did not represent. They kept us, I am sure, out of more than a little mischief, and upon stormy afternoons were worth their weight in gold.

So now, with more prosaic purpose, it was to our blocks that we had recourse, and placing them carefully under each end of the broomstick we raised our bar triumphantly, a block at a time. How I wish that I had the records of those early meets to-day! How I should like to look back at them, and see, at seven, eight and nine years of age, what heights we really cleared! Alas! Our score-sheets, with the badges, the constitution and the by-laws, have vanished forever; treacherous memory is of no avail, and our records, like those of the Olympic Games of old, are shrouded in impenetrable mystery. A chair and a block — a chair and two blocks — if recollection serves me rightly, even three — but of what we accomplished in terms of feet and inches, not a trace remains.

One other memory of the long hallway comes vividly back to me. Those were the days of the pedestrians, and the sport had culminated in those tremendous contests of endurance known, in the sporting phrase, as the "six day go-as-you-please." There always seemed to me a kind of irony about the name, for while in theory the participants were thus left free to follow any gait they chose, only too frequently, as they neared the end of the struggle, the poor wretches, with dizzy heads and staggering limbs, were not only unable to go as they pleased, but were wholly unable to go at all.

One of these races was held in Boston. I went to see it upon the opening day, and after that again and again, for it gripped me with a fascination I could not resist. I cannot remember where the contest was held, but I seem to recall a long, low building, with a board track covered with sawdust; the whole tone of the affair cheap and sordid to a degree, and among the spectators the proper sporting atmosphere of much cheap tobacco and much cheaper slang. Yet I paid little heed to my surroundings; all my interest was in the racers themselves. Footsore and weary, gaunt and grim, they plodded along; walking, running, walking again; not stopping even to eat, but snatching the food from their trainers' hands, and devouring it, as they sped around the track, with no perceptible slackening of their speed. For hour after hour they kept at their task, taxing themselves, as it seemed, to the very uttermost limit; and always, on the huge score board at the end of the hall, their records mounted higher and higher, lap after lap, mile after mile. I can see the whole scene now, as if it had been but yesterday. Names, figures, faces; gestures and tricks of speech; one and all again come crowding to my mind. I can see Guerrero, the swarthy Mexican, picturesque and debonair; Herty and Hegelman; Sullivan, with his pale face and sunken cheeks, and "Old Man" Taylor, the "Pie-eater," plodding wearily along at his steady jog, with his eyes half-closed and his head sunk upon his breast.

Cheap and sordid, as I say, and yet the lesson that I learned there was none the less a noble one. For I was too young to distinguish between amateur and professional, and the commercial side of the enterprise, except as it affected my own pocket, made not the slightest impression upon my mind. But the race itself — the struggle of courage and endurance against hunger, and fatigue, and physical distress — struck me as something *magnificent and fine*. And so I must go home, remove my jacket, knot a handkerchief about my waist, and another (Heaven knows why) about my head, and then walk and trot up and down the hallway, as seriously and with as much determination as if I had been a very champion of champions. My imagination, I think, was at least normally active at the time, for I can remember placing a large, damp sponge upon a chair at the end of the hall, and stopping every few laps to breathe very loudly, and mop my face until it shone; then, in imitation of one or the other of my heroes, I would start away upon my tramp once more.

With these faint memories, the sports of childhood, real and imaginary, fade from my mind. And now, having come to the age of fifteen, I was to make my first real bow to the athletes' world. The occasion was the "junior sports" of my school; the scene was the Readville trotting track; the date May 25, 1889. A faded and tattered programme lies beside me as I write, and many a name, well-known in the business world to-day, looks up at me from the printed page. Running, jumping, throwing the baseball, putting the shot — those were the events, some eight or nine in all. For the sake of comparison, I mention here some of the records of the boys of twenty years ago. The hundred-yards dash was won in $11\frac{1}{2}$ seconds, and the half-mile run in $2\frac{1}{2}$ minutes. The shot weighed 16 pounds; 24 feet and 5 inches was the winning put. The record for the standing broad jump was 8 feet $4\frac{1}{2}$, and for the running broad 17 feet 10. The standing high jump was won at 3 feet 11, and the running high at 4 feet $7\frac{1}{2}$. And if some of these performances, to the boys of to-day, seem to be lacking in merit, it must be remembered that we had no

JAMES S. MITCHELL

one to coach us, no facilities for training, and
that our records were thus made off-hand,
without practice or preparation of any kind.

Of all the boys who competed, I can remember the one who stood forth preëminent
as the best performer of the day. This was
Charles Brewer, who was later to play football at Harvard as a member of the 'Varsity
team. I have seen most of the schoolboy
athletes since his time; some of them, under
the modern system of training, have surpassed
the records which he made; but none, I think,
have possessed the real ability to run and
jump which seemed to be his by nature. He
was a trifle above medium height, slender
rather than stocky; wiry, lithe and active, with
plenty of spring, and as fleet of foot as a deer.
Even at this time, he showed his ability by
winning first in the standing high and running
broad jumps, third in the standing broad, and
second in the baseball and the hundred yards.
His record in the running broad, 17 feet and 10
inches, under conditions which were none of
the best, promised well for the future. And a
year or so later, indeed, he developed won-
derfully, and became New England interscholastic champion at the two hundred and

twenty yards, the broad jump, and the quarter mile. Moreover, while still at school, he won the quarter-mile championship of all New England, and that, too, against the pick of a first-class field. Close to 50 seconds for the quarter, 21 feet and 6 inches in the broad jump — for a schoolboy, practically untrained, these were records little short of marvelous. But on entering college, Brewer turned his attention to football and rowing, and thereafter never again competed with any seriousness upon the track. His fleetness of foot served him well upon the football field, although he hardly had the weight and size for an ideal football man. Nature had designed him for the highest honors as a runner and jumper, and from the standpoint of athletics I have never ceased to regret his retirement from the track. There have been many greater football players than Brewer, but had he devoted himself to his specialties, the men who would have excelled him there might still be numbered, I think, upon the fingers of one's hand.

Another of the day's athletes, who was later to become famous, was Charles J. Paine, Jr. He was tall, strong, and exceptionally rugged, and could make a showing at almost anything he tried. But the high jump was his particular specialty. Long before he entered college, he was a first-class performer, and jumped consistently in the neighborhood of 6 feet. But with the beginning of his college course, like Brewer, his very versatility proved a hindrance to him. Baseball was his hobby; he became a famous pitcher, and played for several years upon the 'Varsity team. Yet he was urgently needed upon the track, as well, and thus every year, a few days before the intercollegiates and the dual games with Yale, he was granted a leave of absence from the nine, came out for a day or two's practice, and with this scanty preparation, went into the contest as if he had been training all the spring, and never emerged save with credit to himself. I remember seeing him, on a cold and rainy day, clear 6 feet and over in the dual games with Yale, and this upon his first attempt, after waiting half an hour or more while the others were deciding a lengthy tie for second place. I am confident that, had he followed the track instead of devoting himself to baseball, he would have cleared 6 feet 2, perhaps even 6 feet 3; and the jumpers who achieve these heights are still few and far between.

My own part in the meet was limited to the standing high jump, where I finished second to Brewer, and the running high jump — the event we had practised so assiduously in the early days of the B. A. C. I entered this latter contest not without hope of success, for I had jumped 4 feet and 4 inches in practice, and, from what I could learn of the ability of the others, judged that this was quite good enough to win. Yet the pastime of reckoning victory and defeat beforehand is a somewhat profitless one, at best. There is the danger of underrating your opponents, and the equal danger of underrating yourself, since in either case, whatever the practice work may have been, the stress of actual competition usually causes the most unexpected results. And thus, while on the day of the sports I cleared the expected 4 feet 4, so also did my friend Paine. In turn we cleared 4 feet 5, and 4 feet 6; and finally, at 4 feet $7\frac{1}{2}$, I was left the victor. Let no one grudge me the joy of thus recording my triumph, for though, in later years, we were to jump against each other more than once, our positions were ever afterwards reversed, and strive as I might, this victory over him was my first — and last.

Thus my first trophy was won. I remember, in passing, that our exchequer that year was extremely low, and that the whole matter of prizes was most difficult of solution. At last we hit upon the expedient of procuring, to begin with, five-cent pieces of the current year. Thus we had our date already inscribed, and after diligent search, and much unsuccessful bargaining, we at length discovered a silversmith, who agreed, at reasonable expense, to shave away the other side of the coin, and to place upon it the name of the event, and of the school. Since then, I believe, such tampering with the currency has been made an indictable offense. I trust it was not so at the time. In any event, if we sinned, it was through ignorance, and the coin hangs in a corner of my medal case to-day, the first, and with some few exceptions, the most valued, of the trophies of twenty years.

And here I would say a word on the whole question of the prize, and its importance to the athlete, for it is a subject on which I believe there is uttered a vast amount of cant. None of us, I suppose, have much sympathy with the "mug-hunter," the man who pursues cups and medals for their own sake, that he may hoard and treasure them, as a miser hoards his gold. Such an ideal of sportsmanship is so wholly bad that we may at once dismiss it, with a shrug of the shoulders; and yet there is another side to the question as well. For the very fear and dread of such a taint leads many a young man into an utter disdain of the prize, sometimes real, more often, I think, affected, but in either case to be deplored. Athletics are, or should be, a pleasure and a diversion, a foil to the more serious affairs of life; and surely, as the years roll on, there is not such a superabundance of joy in the world that even the most cheerful of us are not sometimes glad to refresh ourselves with a glance backward along the way. And here, it is true, it is the bitter memories which are most easily forgotten, the happy ones which answer most readily to our call. Yet memory itself, at its best, is not always to be depended upon; and that which helps us to recall past joys, we should welcome thankfully, not despise and set aside. And thus the sight of a cup or of a medal may bring to life again whole days of glorious sunshine, cities and towns in every part of the world, and best of all, the faces of our friends.

This, at least, is how the matter presents

itself to me; as if to scorn a reminder of past happiness came somehow perilously near to scorning life itself. And yet my view (strangely enough, we all have this experience) is not the wholly accepted one. Let me give two illustrations. I was talking one day with an athlete of rare distinction, who had competed for years with almost unvarying success, and whose name still adorns the columns of the record books. In the course of the conversation, I chanced to express a desire to see the cups that he had won. "Cups?" he half-doubtfully answered, "Why, yes, I think I *have* got two or three barrels of them somewhere. They're packed away in the cellar, I believe." Upon which answer I make no comment, except to wonder whether all the true poetry and charm of sport had ever fairly entered our champion's mind.

The second illustration is this. A young man had won first place in one of the jumping events at the intercollegiate games. All the next year, he was prevented from training, but at the last moment, nevertheless, he elected to defend his title. Among his opponents were two jumpers of exceptional ability from another college. On the first day, when the preliminary round was held, the title-holder was in his accustomed form, qualified without effort for the finals and to all appearance had every prospect of winning his event for the second time. But on the morning of the next day, as he told me later, he knew, in the simple act of walking up-stairs, that the exertion of the preliminaries had tired him, had dulled the fine wire edge of his muscles, and that the spring and ease of his jumping were gone. With the coming of afternoon, his fears proved true. He strove with every artifice in his power. The form of his jump was as fine as ever; his strength in no wise diminished; yet his wearied muscles would not respond, and even as he cleared the lowest height of all, he knew himself foredoomed to defeat. Against an ordinary field, indeed, he might still have won, but not with two such jumpers opposed to him, and with third place he was forced to be content. And when, at the end of the games, he filed up with the others to receive his prize, he took the bronze medal in silence, for a moment gazed grimly down upon it, and then drew back his arm and sent it hurtling through the air, far over the top of the tall grand-stand, where, for anything that I know to the contrary, it still reposes to this day. Upon which action I prefer to make no comment at all, but to leave the reader to deduce the moral, or morals, of the tale, to please himself.

Two other aspects of the question of prizes here present themselves to my mind. First, the value of the trophy; second, of what the trophy itself should consist. In the matter of value, it is no uncommon thing to find contestants openly dissatisfied with the prizes which they have won, and I have known a rebellion among a whole body of athletes, who threatened not to compete at all, unless prizes of a certain value were promised them. The principle underlying all this is too obvious to call for comment, though I confess that if the artistic merit of a prize increased in proportion to its value in dollars and cents, I might sympathize, to some extent, with the rebels, and with their demands. Unfortunately, however, our national taste is not yet a thing proven; and only too often, the more money provided the greater is the opportunity for the designer to magnify his errors upon a larger scale. I have medals among my collection — some, indeed, given at championship meetings —

which are positively an offense to the eye,—
gaudy combinations of color, "fancy" letter-
ing, goddesses attired in the airiest of raiment
bearing huge wreaths of laurel in their out-
stretched hands. And while many of our
medals, notably those of our colleges, do not
deserve to be thus condemned, yet when they
are placed beside the medals of the Olympic
games, the design of a Parisian sculptor, there
is scarcely one which does not fade, upon the
instant, into insignificance. Thus, if money
means beauty, within reasonable limits, I
advocate its use. If not, it seems of no importance, one way or the other.

The question of value apart, of what should
the prize consist? A cup, a medal, a ribbon,
these are all proper; a souvenir, a trophy of
victory — that, and nothing more. Yet every
now and again there springs up a fashion of
giving prizes which may be turned to more
practical account. Umbrellas, bags, lamps,
watches, and the like — all in turn have had
their day. And the spirit which prompts the
givers is, I think, a kindly one. "Our athletes,"
they say, "are not, for the most part, young
men of wealth. After they have won a dozen
cups and medals, what use have they for more?

Let us give them a chance to win something useful instead."

This seems, indeed, at first sight, plausible enough, yet in practice it brings us dangerously near the ranks of the professionals. In the case of the medal or the cup, we are winning something which in the ordinary course of events we should never think of going out and purchasing; while in the case of our useful prizes, we are winning, through the exercise of our muscles and our brains, articles which rank among the ordinary necessities of life, and which we should otherwise find it necessary to pay for in cash. At the very least, the amateur spirit is in danger.

I recall, in this connection, an experience of my own. During a summer spent in England I competed in a set of athletic games. The events were rather to my liking; there was no great competition to be faced; and as a result, I bore away with me the most miscellaneous collection of prizes I have ever seen. Memory serves me but dimly, but I recall, at least, a large wooden clock, a pocket knife, a set of salt cellars, a bogwood pipe, a silver watch, and an order (which I transferred to one of my friends of the afternoon) for five shillings' worth of groceries. And as a natural result, while as a rule I try to preserve my trophies with the utmost care, I think that of all that day's collection the pipe is the only article which remains in my possession to-day. Let a prize, then, be emblematic only, and not the oft-quoted "useful article," which we may go forth and purchase at the nearest department store.

After our "junior sports" I had no further competition for a year. In May, 1890, I took part in the senior games of the school, and was second in the running high jump, improving my record to 4 feet and 11 inches. After this, I competed several times in the New England interscholastic games and, to speak with candor, made a showing that could hardly have been worse. Once, indeed, in the high jump, I finished fourth, which would appear at first sight to be doing fairly well, but the love of truth again compels me to go further and to explain that, besides myself, there were but three other competitors in the event. My ambition, indeed, never faltered. I aimed as high as ever; I yearned; I aspired; but judged by the standard of results, I knew as well as any one that I was a complete and miserable failure.

All this was bad enough, yet worse was to come; and a year later my athletic career, if such it could be called, was brought for the time being to an untimely end. I underwent a physical examination; some defect, real or imaginary, was discovered in the action of my heart, and further exercise was at once forbidden. For a boy of seventeen, half-crazy over athletics, this came pretty near the line of black tragedy; yet it enabled me to prove that my love of sport was not a selfish one. I still went to all the athletic meetings; I still cheered on my schoolmates to the victories I could not share; and, most of all, I took to delving in the record books, to study there the names and the achievements of the great men of the past.

What a list of mighty names I found, since the championships were first held in '76: Myers and Ford, Sherrill and Westing, Owen, Cary, and Brooks, in the sprints; Myers, Dohm, and Downs in the quarter; Myers and Goodwin in the half; Fredericks and George, Conneff and Carter, in the distance runs; Jordan and Copeland in the hurdles; Ford, Pritchard, Hallock, and Nickerson in the high jump; Ford in the broad jump; Baxter in the pole vault;

and in the weights those mighty giants, Lambrecht, Coudon, Queckberner, Mitchell, and Gray.

Among such a list, "fortis Gyas fortisque Cloanthus," it were hard indeed to distinguish; and yet three or four, I think, were always my special heroes. And first of all, among the runners, famous for all time, was the name of L. E. Myers, the man who could run practically any distance, short or long, and run it like a champion of champions, as indeed he was. For most of us one national championship seems worthy of years of endeavor, but Myers accumulated championships, as Scott once said of Byron's manner of writing, with "negligent ease." In 1879 we find him winning the two hundred and twenty yards, the quarter and the half; in 1880 (most marvelous of performances) the same three events as in the year preceding, and the hundred yards as well; in 1881 the hundred, two-twenty and quarter, the last in 49⅘ seconds; and in 1884 the two-twenty, quarter and half. Other championships, records, and notable performances might be added at will; but it is enough, perhaps,.to say that this athlete of thirty years ago still stands to-day, as he stood then, the most

GEORGE R. GRAY

remarkable example of an all-around runner that the modern world has known.

Another of my heroes was Malcolm W. Ford. Pick up the championship list at random, and it is hard to read for any length of time without coming across his name. In 1884, 1885, and 1886, we find him champion at the hundred yards; in '85 and '86, at the two-twenty; in '83 at the high jump; in '83, '84, '85, '86, and '89 at the broad jump; and as if all this were not enough, in '85, '86, '88, and '89, he was champion at the all-arounds (of which more hereafter), the most taxing and thorough test of an athlete's skill anywhere to be found. A marvelous performer, a close student and observer, and a man who loved athletics for their own sake — that was Malcolm Ford.

Nor can I close my chapter without mention of two men whose names, for years, were household words, wherever prowess in athletics was esteemed — Mitchell and Gray. Their reign — Gray with the shot, Mitchell with the hammer and fifty-six — was long and absolutely unquestioned. At many a meeting, I believe, they might have claimed the prize as theirs without laying a hand upon the weights at all, and there would have been none to say them nay. For years, too, their records stood unrivaled. And while no man may reign forever, while youth, in the old sporting phrase, will be served, and while Ralph Rose and Flanagan are our champions to-day, yet to be great in one's time — who may aspire to more? and no two names, I think, will ever add more lustre to the annals of American sport than those of James S. Mitchell and George R. Gray.

CHAPTER II

I ENTERED Harvard University in the fall of 1892. Within a week or so I was given a physical examination, and though I approached the ordeal with many misgivings I emerged with flying colors. The verdict on my health was completely reversed. I was pronounced sound in wind and limb; and forthwith, taking heart of grace, I began once more to practice the high jump, and entered for the event in the fall handicap games. The day was raw and chilly, and I jumped very badly indeed. Yet the other competitors did little better, and with a liberal handicap of five inches, I finished first with an actual jump of 5 feet 2½. I can remember how proud I was of the pewter cup — Heaven knows I had little to be proud of in the jump which won it — so that for a long time I was never weary of studying the seal which adorned it, with the Latin motto "Aeque pede pulsanda tellus," the date of the founding of the Association —

1874 — and ' best of all, the winged foot, which stood for all that I longed to achieve, yet at the same time despaired of accomplishing.

After the Christmas holidays, the track team was formally called together. The candidates were divided into different squads, and for an hour each day worked at the dumb-bells and chest-weights in the gymnasium, practised starting in the baseball cage downstairs, and ran through the different distances on the board track out of doors. The starting was by far the most popular part of the work. The men were lined up in the cage, divided into heats, and with judges and a starter were put through a series of ten-yard sprints. Then the winners of the different heats would run again, and would thus be gradually weeded out, until at last one solitary victor remained. The whole thing furnished just the necessary spice of competition, and kept us from wearying of the chest-weights and dumb-bells, which, after a certain length of time, seem somehow to fail a little of inspiration. Moreover, the work was of real value as practice for quick starting, and many a sprinter, later to do good work upon the track, was first brought into notice by a burst of speed shown in this starting in the cage.

After a time, I made some progress at these short dashes, and at the winter meeting in the Gymnasium I was second in the ten-yards dash, and second in the potato race as well. Incidentally, by this sport of potato racing, there hangs a tale. It came suddenly into favor about this time, flourished for several years, and finally died again. It was a peculiarly exciting contest to watch, and a very taxing one for those who took part in it. At the start was placed a line of milk-cans; in front of each, at two-yard intervals, were strung eight potatoes; and the man who first gathered his row, one at a time, and deposited them safely within the can was adjudged the winner. I have called it a taxing race; perhaps it does not sound so, upon paper; yet if you are doubtful, try it for yourself, and see.

At this potato race I achieved some measure of fame. In the two years in which the sport flourished, I started fourteen times, and won nine firsts, four seconds and one third. And in the process, I was to be made a victim of our national desire to create "world's champions" at will. Thirty-five seconds was considered good time for the race; anything under that was pretty sure to win; but on one occasion, in a match against my chief antagonist, I managed to outdo myself, and finished in $32\frac{4}{5}$, which stood, for some time, as the record. Next morning I awoke to find the papers blazing gorgeously, "Boston Man establishes World's Record for Potato Race!" Heavens above! Here was a sport, but newly come into favor, in one city, in one state of the Union, and as far as I am aware, not practised at that time in any other portion of the civilized world. Yet here I was, most sorely against my will, branded as a "Champion of the World." I had dreamed of fame, but never in this guise. Of course, as was to be expected, I was unmercifully "jollied" by my classmates; my official title was bestowed upon me on all possible — and impossible — occasions; and at last the joke was carried to the point where presentations of potatoes, both real and artificial, were sent me, by express and through the mail. I was powerless, and could do little more than hang my head in shame, yet I have marveled since to find how much company I have had in this special kind of notoriety. If a man cannot contrive in these happy days to become a "world's champion" at one thing or another, it is only because he has no friends —or enemies — among the gentlemen who guide the destinies of that fearful and wonderful thing, our daily press.

Scattered through the different squads of candidates, we could observe those happy beings — the members of the track team of the year before. To us poor novices, they seemed only a little lower than the gods themselves. To possess a sweater with a great white "H" upon it; to possess running-drawers with a crimson stripe down the side; to possess a running-shirt with a crimson band slashed from shoulder to waist, and a small edition of the "H" in the middle — was it any wonder that to us the right to wear that sacred letter seemed, at least for the time being, the very end and justification of existence? For my own part, I shall never forget the awe with which I gazed upon the heroes who had been point-winners in the intercollegiates, or against Yale; and when I thought of what they could do, and then tried to measure my own poor attainments by the side of theirs, I raged inwardly at myself, and alternated between moods of hope (for which there was no justification whatever) and of black despair (for which, looking at the situation coolly and dispassionately, there seemed to be every reason in the world).

And yet, even at this very time, the Fates were conspiring to aid me; a great light was shortly to burst upon my mind; and I was to see at last the entrance to the promised land. Up to now, all the time and labor which I had spent upon athletics had been bestowed with the idea that these sports were a mere question of bone and brawn and muscle, and that the man who happened to be best adapted physically to following them was the man who would defeat all comers. Yet now I was to learn that this theory was untrue or, looked at in the most favorable light, only half true at the most; that skill was greater than strength, brain than muscle; and that the man who once thoroughly mastered the method of performing an event could thereafter hold his own with those infinitely his superiors in strength and size. This illuminating truth was now for the first time to pierce the density of my mind, and whatever measure of success was to come to me was to be due to the following out of this idea.

The manner of my learning was this. Among

the athletes then competing for the B. A. A.
was James E. Morse, a man who had brought
to the study of athletics a keen and observant
mind and a thorough love for all kinds of sport.
He was one of the best high jumpers in the
country — had cleared his 6 feet and over —
and for his weight and size — he was tall, but
slenderly built, and far from rugged — an exceptionally good all-around performer in every
branch of athletics, and a first-class gymnast
as well. Morse was in the wool business and,
as it chanced, was employed by a man who
was one of the best and kindest friends I
have ever known. This friend was well aware
of my ambitions, and one day told me that
he proposed introducing me to Morse, in the
hope that he might give me some advice
of value. It was on the 22d of February,
1893, that the meeting was brought about. I
was jumping at a set of games in the old Tech-
nology Gymnasium, on Exeter Street, and was
performing with my usual enthusiasm, and I
fear, with my usual lack of intelligence. I had,
however, begun to fill out considerably; had
grown taller and broader, and was altogether,
physically, in the best shape of my life. And
so, although my style was as bad as ever, the

result of my added strength had told a little on my jumping, and I was good for about 5 feet 4. I still jumped the old side jump, and was so intent upon getting a good "crouch," as it is technically called, that I approached the bar in a manner which I can now see, as I look back upon it with the conservatism of age, fully merited the derision it always aroused. Even at this set of games, I can remember that one small boy, with the unerring instinct of youth, hit upon the proper word to describe my style. As I came sneaking down towards the bar, very much in what I should conceive to be the manner of a man with a guilty conscience starting out to rob a hen-roost, this young reprobate called out, "Oh, Gee, fellers, look! Here comes the prowler!" Candid friends recognized with delight the aptness of the phrase, and the chance remark blossomed and bore fruit for more years than I care to recall.

With my prowling style, then, I cleared, as usual, my 5 feet 4, and as usual, failed at the succeeding height. Morse watched me carefully, but said never a word until after the games, when he sought me out in the dressing-room. I stood waiting to hear his verdict, like a prisoner about to receive sentence, and not, I think, much more hopefully. "Well," he said at last, "you've plenty of spring," and then, as I remained silent, he went on, not unkindly, "but here's the trouble. You don't know anything about jumping at all. You don't understand the first principles of getting your body over the bar. I could take you and train you, and in six months from now I could have you jumping 5 feet 10."

I gazed at him, incredulous; started to answer, and then stopped. Words were inadequate. If I had heard that in six months I should be fitted to jump over the moon, I should have believed it almost as readily. And still my mind could not help dwelling on his words in a kind of sing-song, "5 feet 10, 5 feet 10"; and when he went on to explain his plans, I fell in with them with the utmost readiness. He was to have a set of standards made, prepare a mat from the bags in the warehouse, and then clear a space in the wool loft, where I could come down two or three times a week for practice. Within a week our lessons began. And any one who has ever learned the wrong way of performing an event, and then turned around and attempted to learn the right one, will know at the outset what I went through. "Jump like this," Morse would say. "Jump like this," my brain would repeat, and then, when I would try to convert theory into practice, my unruly muscles would interfere and spoil everything by continuing as they had always done.

At last, after much patient teaching on Morse's part and after much blundering effort on my own, I reached the point where I could clear about 5 feet and 7 inches. There seemed, if I could do this in the spring games, just the faintest chance that I could make the team. There was competition in plenty. G. R. Fearing, Jr., of the class of 1893, was then a senior, and was not only by all odds the best high jumper in college, but by an equal margin the best in all the colleges as well. Four years in succession he was champion at the intercollegiates — a feat in that event never duplicated. And if there is any other branch of athletics which Fearing has been unable to master, I have yet to learn of it. He was (and is) a notable figure in the world of sport. Runner, jumper, hurdler, oarsman, player of tennis and racquets — I will not prolong the list to weariness. A more versatile performer, I think, never lived. There was something almost irritating, not in his success, but in the manner in which he achieved it. What others had to toil and scheme and plan to accomplish, he simply came out and did. I may, after so many years, be in error; there may have been the deepest method under the apparent carelessness of his work; but to all outward appearance, it looked as if he essayed a thing, and with his combination of strength and agility, could not miss it if he tried. Professor Saintsbury has told us of the hapless critic who profoundly observed that Scott's originality could not be considered in his favor, since it came to him by nature. And in much the same way, to those of us who had to work hard and long finally to achieve our little measure of success, it seemed as if Fearing's ability was so entirely a matter of course that he deserved no credit for the wonders which he achieved.

Besides Fearing, we had for high jumpers T. E. Sherwin and G. C. Chaney, both of the class of '94, and W. E. Putnam, Jr., a classmate of my own. Sherwin, at that time, was the best of the three, jumping consistently around 5 feet 8 or 9. Chaney was a man who possessed great natural advantages, to begin with. He was 6 feet and 6 inches in height, and had a somewhat unstudied style of jumping, running directly at the bar, and tucking his legs up under him in the manner of Con Leahy and the other great Irish jumpers. As it so happened, he never did his best work in college competition; but, by the irony of fate, no sooner was he graduated than I saw him enter an unimportant meeting on the old Irvington Oval, and with the utmost ease go on clearing height after height until he had gone over 5 feet 11¾. This, indeed, is one of the hardships of athletics. A song much in vogue a few years ago had for its refrain, "It's seldom or never you'll find them together,—the time, and the place, and the girl." And to paraphrase this for the athlete, it is seldom or never that the combination of the right day, the right opportunity and the top-notch of condition all work together to result in a truly great performance.

Putnam was in every way a complete contrast to Chaney. He was of medium height, lithe and slender, an excellent gymnast, and a most graceful and scientific jumper. He took a long run at the bar with his distance accurately divided and measured, and his "layout" as he jumped was so good — his body so nearly parallel to the ground — that more than once, with the bar up around 5 feet 9 or 10, I have seen him apparently over in safety, only at the very last moment of all to knock it off with the very back of his head.

Thus I had competitors in plenty, and, as might well have been expected, I did not succeed in making the team. In the class games, Fearing did not compete. His place upon the team was too well assured to call for any display of his powers. Sherwin won at 5 feet $8\frac{1}{4}$, and Chaney, Putnam, and myself tied for second at 5 feet 7. Then in the long jump-off I failed, and the others were successful. And as the last straw, in my final desperate effort I managed somehow to spike myself severely, cutting a long clean gash just above the ankle and extending half way in to the bone. Altogether, I limped off the field, feeling that the world was a place of deepest gloom, and that all the time and trouble which my friend Morse had spent upon me had been wholly thrown away.

In reality, however, I think that my failure to do better in the spring games was largely due to a mixture of overtraining and of over-anxiety to do well. For after a rest, in August of that same year, at the City of Cambridge games, I distinguished myself in most un-looked-for fashion. The games had a notable entry list, the New York Athletic Club sending over a team, among whom were Goff, the all-around champion, "Tommy" Conneff, the champion at the mile, and a number of others. Holmes Field was the scene of competition; the day was perfection; and altogether it was a good chance for any one to do his best. I was entered, as usual, in the high jump, and felt vaguely, as I cleared the lower heights, that I seemed to have an unusual amount of spring. I cleared 5 feet 8 without trouble, the best performance I had ever shown; and then 5 feet 9. At 5 feet 10, I failed twice, just displacing the bar at each attempt; but, on my last trial, with a tremendous wriggle I worked clear of the bar, and with my handicap of four inches was a safe winner over the rest of the field. It was on the whole rather a singular vindication of Morse's judgment. He had found me jumping 5 feet 4 and had said that in six months he could add 6 inches to my jump; and now, six months later, almost to the

THOMAS P. CONNEFF

day, I made good his prediction, and to the very fraction of an inch.

One good jump, however, does not make a jumper. The next spring I again managed to overtrain, and to my disgust, once more failed to make the team. But in the fall of my junior year I began at last to amount to something. I had taken up the broad jump, shot and hammer, and had shown some proficiency in all three. I was good for 21 feet and over in the broad, could put the shot about 38 feet, while with the hammer I threw over 120 feet, and broke the Harvard record. The following spring I made the team, and with that out of the way, my next ambition was to win a point in the games with Yale, and thus have the right to wear my "H." Yet ill-luck was still to be my portion. On the day of the games, I competed in the broad jump, and the high. In the broad, it was conceded that Sheldon, of Yale, and Stickney, of Harvard, would share first and second, but I had strong hopes of third. One of the Yale jumpers, a slight, sandy-haired young man named Mitchell, was to upset my calculations. He came out for his first trial, and to my horror, cleared 21 feet and 7 inches. I came next, and had the agony of hearing my jump announced as 21 feet 6¾. Neither of us could better these first attempts, and Sheldon won, with Stickney second, and Mitchell third. Years afterward, Mitchell and I chanced to meet again, for the first time since that day, and as we shook hands, we both smiled. "I think," said he, "that we've met before. "I think," I responded, "that I still remember a little matter of a quarter of an inch," and forthwith, with much good feeling, we talked over the old times, and the events which had appeared to us then of more importance, perhaps, than anything else in the world.

Thus I was shut out in the broad jump; and I was to be unsuccessful in the high as well. Paine of Harvard was the winner, and Putnam of Harvard, Thompson of Yale and myself were tied for second at 5 feet 9½. On the long jump-off both the others finally cleared the next height, and I was the one to fail. 21 feet 6¾ in the broad — 5 feet 9½ in the high — and not even a third place to show for it. It was sufficiently discouraging.

And now, after all my troubles, my fortune was at length to change; 1897, from start to finish, was to be my lucky year. Our first contest of the spring was with Pennsylvania, and there was more than usual interest in the outcome of the games. For one thing, we had beaten them the year before, at Philadelphia, and they were looking for their revenge. Besides this, both teams were good ones and so evenly matched that to pick a winner seemed little better than guesswork. In the sprints we had Bigelow, Roche and Denholm, all three running close to even time, while they had a new-comer named Hoffman whom they claimed for a certain winner, both in the hundred and two-twenty. We felt sure of the quarter and half, with Hollister; they were equally certain of the mile, with the famous Orton, and the walk, with Fetterman. "Billy" Morse was our hope in the low hurdles, and many of us believed that he could even defeat J. D. Winsor, Jr., the Pennsylvania captain, in the high jump as well. We figured on the broad jump, with J. G. Clark, while word came to us from Philadelphia that we need not worry over that event, as J. P. Remington, their best man, was clearing 23 feet in practice, and was absolutely not to be beaten for first. They conceded us the pole-vault, with Hoyt, while in the weights we had to acknowledge that with Woodruff and McCracken, the famous football players, they would have practically a clean sweep both in the hammer and the shot. Altogether, it gave promise of being as close and exciting a meeting as one could wish to see.

From these games, it so chanced that I was to gain something of a reputation for "making good" in a tight place, while as a matter of fact, the only credit I deserved was for doing a lot of hard work — apparently without hope of reward — in practising with the shot. This, however, appears to be one of life's many puzzles, as well as one of its somewhat cynical consolations. We are blamed for many things of which we are not guilty, and in return, obtain credit for much to which we have no shadow of a claim.

The affair of the shot-put came about in this wise. The managers of the team, realizing our weakness in the event, announced a series of competitions, with the idea of developing some one who might possibly at the utmost pick up a single point in the games. There is really no better plan with the hammer and shot than holding frequent competitions of this kind. Not only does it arouse interest, but in addition there are no other events in which the competitors are so apt to fall short of their practice form. Unconsciously, a man is apt to acquire the habit of taking twenty or thirty trials with the shot and hammer, and of regarding the best throw of all as the distance which he is really capable of accomplishing. In a sense of course this is true; but when he faces actual competition, he has as a rule no chance for any great amount of preliminary "warming-up"; he has his three trials within the narrow compass of a seven-foot circle; and if he makes a foul throw his effort goes for naught. Thus there is little to be wondered at if a man fails to equal his practice throws, and the discipline of frequent competition is the only thing to show him what he may fairly count upon doing in the actual contest itself.

We had plenty of fun that winter out of this practice, but our performances were nothing more than fair. I won the prize, as I remember it, for the best average in the series; somewhere between 37 and 38 feet. This, indeed, in itself and for those days was almost respectable, but compared with the records of our rivals it was hopelessly bad; so that we made up our minds that in the shot-put, at least, we had no faintest shadow of a chance.

The day of the meet came at last, dawning fair and clear,— one of the days that I shall always remember. The games were held on Holmes Field, that spot so rich in associations and memories. Never, to me at least, and I am sure to many others as well, can there be another field to take its place: the dark oval of the track, circling the green of the diamond; nearer the college yard, the well-rolled jumping-paths; and beyond them, just at the curve leading into the stretch, that famous spot, beneath the towering willows, where many a man has moved gamely up through his field, making his final effort in the quarter-mile. The Stadium of to-day is magnificent, its track superb; but between it and old Holmes Field there is the same difference as between some splendid castle, which you are glad to visit for a time, and the peace and comfort of your home. Field, track, jumping-paths,— all are gone, but the heritage of the past remains; and around the spot there linger still the memories of mighty contests, of the great athletes of the past, of victories won for one's college, not for self, and best of all, win or lose, of sport that has been always fair and clean.

We dressed that day in the old Carey Building across the field, and sat there waiting when the call was given for the first heat in the high hurdles. The moment when we rose and sauntered slowly across to the start is as clear in my mind as if it had happened yesterday. To the athlete, trained to the minute, the freedom of his limbs scarce hampered by his light running-clothes, breathing the pure air, feeling the warm sun beating down upon him, there comes the splendid sensation of *living*, the feeling of strength and power equal to the best. And then, just before the start, to hear the band come crashing to its close, and in the hush that follows to hear the three long Harvards, the three times three, and one's name at the end; then, indeed, each nerve and muscle seem strung to tensest strain; whatever mortal man can do — to that one feels that he may attain.

Fortune at the start favored us. In the first heat of the hurdles, Hallowell, of Harvard, and myself were drawn with two Pennsylvania men. I won in $16\frac{2}{5}$, with Hallowell second. And in the next heat, Fox, our best man, won, with Williams of Harvard again beating out the Pennsylvanians. It was a good beginning, and we postponed the finals until later, a day or two after the meet. Fox won, I was second, and Hallowell third.

The hundred came next, and I scarcely remember a more exciting race. Bigelow won the first heat in 10⅖, with Denholm second. Hoffman had been drawn in the second heat, and we watched him anxiously, as he jogged down the track before the start, eager to see if he measured up to the standard that was claimed for him. He looked dangerous, beyond a doubt. He was tall, rangy and muscular, and covered the ground easily with a long and powerful stride. He took the lead at the start and won his heat in ten seconds flat, with Roche of Harvard a good second, so that he was left the only Pennsylvanian in the final, with the three fastest Harvard runners against him. And what a race the final was, — how painfully dramatic its ending! At 90 yards, Roche, fairly outdoing himself, was in the lead, and all bias aside, I think, at least as I viewed the race, would have won. And then — with the tape almost in his grasp, in one sudden instant a tendon failed him and, wholly helpless, he pitched forward headlong upon the track, leaving Hoffman to flash past the line a winner, with Bigelow second and Denholm third. And still, our sympathy for Roche aside, we were not unduly cast down, for from the very first we had not been over-confident of the sprints; and when a moment later we won all three places in the quarter, with Hollister, Vincent, and Fish, we felt that our chances still looked bright. Then Hollister won the half, in 1.57$\frac{2}{5}$; Morse won the low hurdles, and Hoyt the pole vault; and then the luck shifted strongly in the opposite direction. Hoffman, as we had expected, won the two-twenty; Fetterman won the walk; and in the mile not only did Orton win, as every one knew he would, but Pennsylvania took the other two places as well. The high jump was a battle royal. Both Morse and Winsor cleared 6 feet and 1 inch, and then Winsor got over 6 feet 2$\frac{1}{2}$, the best individual performance of the day. The broad jump, too, went against us. J. G. Clark cleared 22 feet 3$\frac{3}{4}$, and I did 22 feet and $\frac{1}{4}$ inch; but Remington, with a jump of 22 feet 8, defeated us both. Woodruff and McCracken were first and second in the hammer, and we came to the last event, the shot-put, with the score 55 to 49 in Harvard's favor. Here, however, Pennsylvania was counting on winning all three places and the games. I remember that deep down in my heart I had all along felt that I had a chance for third, for my practice putting had been very consistently in the neighborhood of 38 feet. I made my first put slow and sure, and put exactly 38 feet to an inch. McCracken's first put was the best of the day, 40 feet $6\frac{1}{2}$ inches, and Woodruff, who was bothered with a lame hand, made 40 feet and $\frac{1}{4}$ inch. And then on my third put I caught things right; I knew as the shot left my hand that I had outdone myself. There was a little pause as the knot of officials gathered about the tape, and then the measurer rose and called out, "40 feet $4\frac{1}{4}$ inches." We had won second place, and with it the games themselves, by the narrowest of margins, 57 to 55.

One incident that followed I like especially to recall. I had taken a car for home, and midway over the Harvard Bridge the coach bearing the Pennsylvania team swept by. I was standing upon the rear platform of the car; some one on the coach saw me, and the next instant, to my infinite surprise, I was honored for the first and only time in my life with the Pennyslvania cheer, with my name at the end.

When I hear people talk of the need of clean sport and the lack of the amateur spirit, I like to look back upon the games with Pennsylvania and recall that cheer.

CHAPTER III

COLLEGE DAYS — HEROES PAST AND PRESENT — THE RUNNERS

COLLEGE athletics — the specialized and systematized athletics of to-day — are such a recent growth that the historical background is of necessity almost wholly lacking. The great athletes of the seventies and eighties occupy a kind of dubious middle ground. On the one hand, their records are just old enough to be unfamiliar to the present generation; on the other, their deeds have not as yet been fittingly told or sung, and the halo of antiquity does not as yet surround their brows. Thus the effect upon their fame is to cause it to grow dim, and the modern youth is apt to dismiss the name of some great athlete of the past with an incisive — "Never heard of him; what the devil did *he* ever do, anyway?" To recall the performances of some of these worthies, now dangerously near oblivion, as well as to comment upon some of the college heroes of to-day, is the purpose of this chapter.

In the sprints, the first name of prominence is that of H. H. Lee, of Pennsylvania, who won the hundred yards in 1877, '78 and '79; and in the first-named two years the two-twenty, as well. His best record for the hundred, $10\frac{1}{5}$, shows how slight the improvement in time has been, over a period of thirty years.

Lee's direct successor was Evart Wendell, of Harvard, who won the two-twenty in 1879, the hundred and the two-twenty in 1881, and in 1880 accomplished the remarkable feat of winning the hundred, two-twenty and quarter, all in the same afternoon. After Wendell came H. S. Brooks, Jr., of Yale, who won the hundred in 1882 and in 1884, both times in $10\frac{1}{5}$; and who won the two-twenty in 1882 and 1883, on the first occasion in the very fast time, for those days, of $22\frac{2}{5}$. Then came Wendell Baker, of Harvard, who won the two-twenty for three years in succession, and in 1885 captured the quarter as well; and to Baker succeeds the famous name of C. H. Sherrill, of Yale, who won the hundred (the only man to accomplish the feat) for four years in succession, beginning in 1887 and ending in 1890. His time for the four years was $10\frac{2}{5}$; $10\frac{3}{5}$; $10\frac{1}{5}$; $10\frac{2}{5}$; a very high and very consistent order of sprinting; and in every year but the first he also won the two-twenty, his time being $22\frac{3}{5}$, $22\frac{2}{5}$ and $22\frac{1}{5}$. It seemed indeed as if such work as this would stand a long time upon the record books, and yet the very next year appeared the phenomenal L. H. Cary, of Princeton, who broke all college records by running the hundred in 10 seconds flat and the two-twenty in $21\frac{4}{5}$. Then Swayne and Richards of Yale and Ramsdell of Pennsylvania each held the championship for a year, both in the shorter and the longer dash, Ramsdell equaling Cary's time of 10 seconds for the hundred, and both Swayne and Ramsdell running the two-twenty in 22 seconds flat.

The next year, 1895, was to see a new champion, this time from the West — John V. Crum, of the University of Iowa. I recall that for some little time before the intercollegiates of that year we heard great things of Crum, but were rather inclined to shrug our shoulders and give scant credit to the times he was reputed to have made. Yet on the day of the games, he convinced the most skeptical among us by winning both dashes in impressive form and duplicating Ramsdell's feat of the year previous by running them both in even time. A year or so later we were shocked to hear of Crum's death. I can remember no other athlete who made friends more readily or won greater respect for the sterling qualities of his character. I have always remembered with pleasure the story one of my classmates told me of the start of the two-twenty on the final day of the games. He was standing near the line, and observed Crum digging the holes which each sprinter makes in the track to enable him to get a firmer and quicker start in the dash. The Western man was using a knife of a design unfamiliar to my friend, and stepping up to Crum he asked him if there was any special virtue in its use. Crum looked up at him with a smile. "I got it," he answered, "from an old man that keeps a shoemaker's shop out home. He asked me to bring it on with me when I came East to tackle you chaps, and to be sure to use it, so that I'd get my start right anyway, no matter how I finished." And five minutes later he had demonstrated to the satisfaction of every one that he could finish as well as start.

Crum remained in the East all that summer, for this was the year of the international games between England and America, and for a long time he was looked upon as our mainstay against the English sprinters. And yet before the games were held another man was to make his appearance, a man greater even than Crum, and one who at his best was, I believe, the greatest all-around sprinter the country has ever seen. This was Bernard J. (better known as "Bernie") Wefers, who hailed from Georgetown in his college days, and later on ran in the colors of the New York Athletic Club. Wefers had been running in the meets around Boston for a number of years, and was rated as a fast man, although he had never had the benefit of systematic training, and was never, I think, quite in the very top-notch of physical condition. I remember competing against him in the hundred at the games of the Gloucester Athletic Club on Decoration Day, in 1895. He was on scratch, and with a handicap of five yards and a half I managed to beat him in the final heat by a very narrow margin. Shortly after this, he went to Travers Island to train under "Mike" Murphy for the games with the Englishmen, and what a transformation a few weeks wrought in him! I went on that year to compete at the national championships in September, and the first man to come up and shake hands with me was Wefers. He was brown as an Indian, the very picture of health, and moved up and down the track as if he were set on springs. His first words were, "$5\frac{1}{2}$ yards would n't do you any good to-day"; and as I watched him beat his field, Crum included, in both the hundred and two-twenty, I felt that he could have given me 10 yards and a beating as easily as 5. He repeated his victories over the Englishmen, and the next spring ran at the intercollegiates and not only won the hundred in $9\frac{4}{5}$, breaking the record, but achieved the really marvelous distinction of winning the two-twenty in $21\frac{1}{5}$ seconds, a record still unbeaten, and never equaled until the intercollegiates of 1910, when R. C. Craig, of Michigan, astonished every one by running the distance in the same wonderful time of $21\frac{1}{5}$.

After Wefers, Tewksbury of Pennsylvania proved a worthy successor, winning both dashes in 1898 and 1899 and making the same excellent time in both years, 10 seconds in the hundred, and $21\frac{3}{5}$ in the two-twenty.

In 1900 we find the name of an athlete who was a first-class performer in more different events than any other man who has so far appeared upon the athletic stage. This is a broad and sweeping statement, but I make it advisedly and with the necessary emphasis upon the words "first-class." To-day, we have a wonderful performer in all-around work in the person of Martin Sheridan; but his development is so perfect and so even in all the different events that, with the exception of the discus, where he reigns supreme, he never shows his real strength outside of the actual competition for the all-around championship. In any other championship meeting there are always two or three men who can defeat him in any one event — specialists opposed to an athletic "general practitioner"; but the man of whom I am now to speak could go out in any company and be absolutely certain of two events, practically certain of a third, and in two or three others was all but the equal of the best. And thus the follower of athletic history needs hardly to be told that the name of this great performer was Alvin C. Kraenzlein, of Pennsylvania.

Kraenzlein was the greatest individual champion of the intercollegiates. He competed for three years, 1898, 1899 and 1900, and no man could have made a more dramatic entrance

ALVIN C. KRAENZLEIN

upon the intercollegiate stage than he did in
the first-named year. Up to that time he was
one of the many "great unknowns" who occasionally make good all the reports of their
prowess, but who much more often when
faced with men of real championship timber
fail utterly to sustain their paper reputation.
At Pennsylvania, indeed, they knew what a
find they had made, but in Cambridge, and I
think in the other colleges as well, every one
was disposed to ridicule the stories of a man
who was breaking world's records in practice
merely by way of ordinary, every-day diversion. Our awakening came in a manner never
to be forgotten. Four years before, J. L. Bremer, Jr., of Harvard, had been the foremost
low hurdler of his time. Bremer was a first-
class athlete. He was tall, spare and sinewy,
could run a hundred yards in $10\tfrac{4}{5}$ and a
quarter in 51, and for three years in succession won the low hurdles at the intercollegiates, — incidentally, in 1895, establishing a
world's record of $24\tfrac{3}{5}$ seconds for the distance.
After this, he entered the medical school, and
under the pressure of work there gave up
athletics altogether. With the approach of the
intercollegiates of 1898 the Harvard coaches,

worrying over the reports that Pennsylvania had the greatest hurdler who had ever worn a shoe, suddenly awoke to the fact that Bremer had still another year in which he was eligible to represent Harvard on the track. He was at once approached, and finally, solely for the sake of the college, consented at some personal sacrifice of his own time to run. At once we began openly to exult. "There," we remarked with intense self-satisfaction, "perhaps that won't stop a little of this Kraenzlein talk for a while." And yet, to our surprise — even to our amazement — our friends in Philadelphia refused to "scare." And the next word that came to us was that they heartily welcomed Bremer's return to the track, that Kraenzlein would be pleased to meet him, and that their man could beat ours, in the slang of the day, "half the length of a city block."

Thus for the time being our confidence was a little shaken; yet we rallied quickly, discounting the stories we heard on the theory that they were the exaggerations of undergraduates' talk; and when, a week or so before the games, Bremer went through the distance in record time, our courage returned and we could see nothing but victory ahead. Neither, however, could Pennsylvania. It was a repetition of the old problem of the irresistible force and the immovable body. Neither man could lose.

The race, of course, is ancient history now. It was a case of a good man, and a better. Bremer had speed; Kraenzlein was speedier. Bremer had spring; Kraenzlein was springier still. Bremer was strong and active; Kraenzlein was not only his equal, but his superior. And added to all this, Kraenzlein was the first man to run the hurdles in what is now the accepted modern style, not with a bend of the knee and a gathering of the body, but clearing the hurdles stiff-legged, precisely as though he were taking them in his natural stride, — as if they did not exist at all.

There could be, of course, but one result. Bremer ran a race equal to the best he had ever done — and was beaten a full 10 yards. Yet, when the time was given out, it must have blunted the sting of defeat. Kraenzlein had removed from the world's record, not $\frac{1}{5}$ of a second or $\frac{2}{5}$, but an entire second itself. He had covered the distance in $23\frac{3}{5}$. Nothing remained to be said. A new champion had arisen, and a new school of hurdling as well.

In 1898 Kraenzlein won the high and low

hurdles. In 1899 he repeated this performance, and won the broad jump besides, with the record distance of 24 feet 4½ inches. And in 1900, to return to the point whence we started, he made the unequaled record of winning the hundred yards, the high hurdles, the low hurdles, and of finishing second in the broad jump to Meyer Prinstein, his one great rival in that event, — three firsts and a second, in these days of the most intense specialization, against the pick of all the colleges. It is scarcely safe to venture on prophecy in these days of great athletes and great performances, yet I cannot bring myself to believe that Kraenzlein's feat will be equaled for many and many a year.

In the official records of the next three years as they stand to-day, we find in the hundred yards the names of the men who finished second, and a brief note explaining that the name of the winner has been stricken from the records. All this, of course, refers to the affair of Arthur Duffey, of Georgetown, who competed for many years as an amateur, and was acknowledged to be the fastest short-distance man in the country. He won for these three years at the intercollegiates, and made his world's record (now disallowed) of $9\frac{3}{5}$ seconds, in the race of 1902. After all this he competed abroad, fell under suspicion of not being strictly within the amateur fold, and at last, when charged with professionalism, openly admitted the fact, acknowledged that he had for years been deriving support from his "amateur" athletics, and excused himself on the ground that not only were there many others in the same class with himself who lacked the courage to come forward and confess, but that, worse than this, most of the prominent athletic clubs secretly encouraged such practices and were only too glad to secure the presence of prominent athletes, "drawing cards," by the payment of very liberal money for "expenses of travel, etc."

As far as the facts go, Mr. Duffey has spoken from an inside knowledge of the game as it has been played; and from my own experiences, and from the many talks which I have had on the subject with other athletes, past and present, who have been prominent in their day, I believe that he has done no more than speak the truth. It is not perhaps to be wondered at. It is only another instance of our great national failing, one more "sign of the times."

In politics, honesty is sacrificed to success; in business, there is a code of morals scarcely in accord with the teachings of the New Testament; why should our athletics, which we take so seriously, escape the blight? Let us have our world's records, our great athletes, our crowds to come and see them perform; and if, to accomplish all this, we have to sacrifice a little common honesty, a little of somebody's money, and a little of somebody else's self-respect, why, is not the satisfaction of contemplating the splendid result worth the price we pay?

Thus the devil's advocate. And in reply to him we can only say that if there is one place in the world where corruption should not be allowed to enter, it is in the field of amateur sport; and in the case of Mr. Duffey, with his perfectly natural plea, "The others do it too," we can only answer that two wrongs never yet made a right, and we can feel only regret that an athlete who won so many famous races, and who showed so many good qualities during the whole of his racing career, could not have managed to come out squarely as a professional and tried his fortune if he so desired in that open field, instead of competing and winning his fame under the cloak of the spurious "amateur."

After Duffey, Schick of Harvard won the hundred and two-twenty in 1904 and 1905, in the first-named year running the hundred in even time, and the two-twenty in the very remarkable figures of 21⅗, only a fifth behind Wefers' wonderful record. Schick, a truly great sprinter, shares with Wefers the collegiate record of 9⅘ for the shorter dash.

For the next three years, Cartmell, of Pennsylvania, won both dashes, in 1907 running the hundred in even time, and the two-twenty in 21⅘. Then followed Foster, of Harvard, who came into prominence as a first-class man only in the spring of 1909, but who won both the hundred and two-twenty at the intercollegiates, the hundred in 10⅕, and the two-twenty in 21⅗. In 1910, "Tex" Ramsdell, of Pennsylvania, won the hundred in even time, and Craig of Michigan, as already noted, won the two-twenty in 21⅕.

Coming to the quarter-milers, the first name to arrest our attention is that of W. H. Goodwin, Jr., of Harvard. For three years in succession, beginning with 1882, Goodwin won both the quarter and the half, and in 1883 made the remarkable time, for those days, of 51⅕ for the quarter, and 2 minutes and 2 seconds for the half.

Next after Goodwin, Wendell Baker won the quarter in 1885, and then S. G. Wells, also of Harvard, won for three years in succession. In 1889 and 1890 we find the names of two great runners, W. C. Dohm of Princeton and W. C. Downs of Harvard, both of whom were champions at the quarter, and the half as well. Dohm won the quarter the first year in 50 seconds flat, and Downs the half in 2.02⅗, while the year following Downs won the quarter in 50⅘, and Dohm won the half in the remarkable time of 1.57⅕.

The next year — 1891 — produced a new champion and record-breaker in G. B. Shattuck of Amherst, who won in 49½. Then four Harvard men — Wright, Sayer, Vincent and Merrill — each held the title for a year, all four winning their races in better than 51. Merrill was a wonderful performer — one of the half-dozen really great quarter-milers in this country — although his name is probably not so widely known as that of many another man whom he could have defeated with ease. This was because Merrill, like many other great athletes, confined his interest in athletics to his college days and strictly to his college running, not caring to represent either his university or some athletic club in outside competition. He was the most deceptive man to see coming across the field before a race that I remember. He looked heavy, slow, stolid, — really, as the expression goes, as if he "had n't speed enough to get out of his own way"; but when the pistol sounded, what a marvelous change! I can see him now, in his best races on Holmes Field. Half way up the back stretch, he would be running perhaps fifth or sixth, and then, so easily and gradually that you could scarcely realize it, that long, sweeping stride would pick up man after man, until, rounding the turn by the willows, he would have a commanding lead, the battle for first place would be over, and the interest would centre only in the fight for second and third places.

Merrill has left behind him no actual record in black and white to show what he was really capable of doing in the matter of time; but in one of his relay races, where he was the last man upon his side to run, he was caught by separate timing better than 49 seconds, and this, I think, is a fair estimate of what he could do at his best.

The next great name after Merrill's — his equal at the quarter itself, and his superior as an all-around runner — is that of Thomas E. Burke. Burke's name appears in the inter-collegiate records as winner of the quarter in 1896 and 1897 and of the half in 1899. Yet his college running was the least part of his activities. He was a seasoned campaigner, running all distances from the short sprints to the half-mile, and at one time or another adding to his list practically all known championships — interscholastic, dual, intercollegiate, New England, metropolitan, Canadian, national, international and Olympic. Not only was he a great racer, invariably to be depended upon in actual competition, but his records show that he made the most of the advantages that were his by nature. He was tall and slim, yet wiry and rugged at the same time, and his stride in the quarter was enormous. And yet, with all the championships he won and all the records he made, I have always had the impression about Burke's performances that never, even then, was he really forced to his limit. Very possibly I am wrong; often the athlete himself knows better what his capabilities are than the critics who stand and look on at his work — and whether or not Burke ever let himself out to the very last notch or not, his record, as it stands, is so good that it places him in the very front rank of American runners — an all-around racer of the same type and class as L. E. Myers.

The next famous name in the list of quarter-mile champions is that of M. W. ("Maxey") Long of Columbia. Long won the quarter, in 1899, in the very fast time of 49⅖, and the next year, running in the colors of the New York Athletic Club, established the two records which stand to-day, 47 seconds flat for the straightaway quarter, and 47⅘ for the quarter around a turn. Long was perhaps hardly as graceful a runner to watch as some of the other fast quarter-milers, but as some one said of Dixon, the negro pugilist, when at the beginning of his career he was knocking out man after man who ventured to oppose him, "George may not be clever, but he's damned effective." And thus Long, with his great speed and stamina, with his pluck and gameness, though seemingly lacking that last perfection of grace possessed by some, was nevertheless marvelously "effective," as his records prove.

To Long, in 1900, succeeded Dexter Boardman of Yale, a very fast man, who won in $49\frac{3}{5}$; and to Boardman, in turn, succeeded W. J. Holland of Georgetown, who won for the next two years in succession, the second year in the same time that Boardman had made, $49\frac{3}{5}$. Holland was not only a great quarter-miler, but a very good all-around athlete as well. He was among the fast men of his day at 40 yards, a sure $10\frac{4}{5}$ man in the hundred, could make a showing with the weights, and was a good high jumper, broad jumper, and hurdler. In 1897 he competed in the all-around championship of New England, and won second place.

The last great name among the college quarter-milers is that of J. B. Taylor, the colored runner from Pennsylvania, whose death occurred only two years ago. He won the quarter-mile in 1904, 1907, and 1908, and in 1907 established the intercollegiate record of $48\frac{1}{5}$. Of all the runners whom I have ever seen, absolutely without exception, Taylor had the most graceful and the most finished style. Merrill's stride was long and easy, but you could see the effort which made it so; Burke and Long "ran all over," as the saying goes, and as you watched them you were conscious of the power they displayed, and instinctively your hands would clench as if you were running the race with them. But with Taylor, when the pistol sounded and he leaped away into that long, sweeping stride, it was precisely as if some lever had been pressed, some spring released, and a piece of mechanism, perfectly adjusted, on the instant set in motion. It was so natural, so wholly without friction or apparent effort, that as you watched him your muscles, instead of tightening, would relax, and looking at him as he circled the track, you could feel yourself wondering what difficulty people found in running after all. Burke, Long, Taylor — perhaps among so many first-class men these three names stand forth preëminent among the college champions at the quarter-mile.

Coming to the next event — the half — we find that in speaking of the quarter we have already dealt with a number of the half-milers as well — Goodwin, Dohm, and Downes, — men who were prominent, not only in one event, but in both. After the first dozen years of the intercollegiates, the improvement in time is very marked. In 1876 the race was won in 2.16½, and the year following in 2.20½, but after 1890, when Dohm made the remarkable record of 1.57⅛, Wright of Yale, Turner of Princeton, and Corbin of Harvard, each of whom held the title for a year, ran their races faster than two minutes flat.

In 1894, C. H. Kilpatrick of Union College was the winner, and the next year he should have repeated his victory but was outgeneralled by Hollister of Harvard, a fast half-miler, indeed, but scarcely in Kilpatrick's class. Hollister, however, was the better sprinter of the two, and setting an easy pace, managed to beat Kilpatrick in the final sprint in the slow time (slow for these men) of an even two minutes. Later that year, Kilpatrick, running for the New York Athletic Club against the Englishmen, established his great record of 1.53⅘, which stood until 1909, when Lunghi, in the Canadian championships at Montreal, lowered Kilpatrick's time to 1.52⅘.

In 1898 J. F. Cregan of Princeton, better known as a miler, accomplished the feat of winning both the half and the mile, the half in 1.58⅘, and the mile in 4.23⅘ — a truly remarkable performance. The year following, Burke won, and after this no especially noteworthy name occurs until 1904, when E. B. Parsons of Yale won in the fast time of 1.56$\frac{4}{5}$, and the year following, repeating his victory, made the intercollegiate record of 1.56 flat.

In 1907, Haskins of Pennsylvania duplicated Cregan's performance of 1898, by winning both the half and the mile, and in time even more remarkable than Cregan's, running the half in 1.57$\frac{4}{5}$, and the mile in 4.20$\frac{3}{5}$. And in 1909 Paull of Pennsylvania, after breaking the record for the mile, ran also in the half, and although his team-mate, Beck, was the winner, in the fast time of 1.56$\frac{3}{5}$, every one who saw the race agreed that if Paull had so desired, he had the half itself, and the record as well, completely at his mercy. In 1910, however, Paull showed a reversal of form and was defeated by G. H. Whitely of Princeton, in 1.57 flat.

The history of the mile has been much like that of the half — steady improvement from the beginning down to the present day. Some of the early records almost excite a smile — 5.33 in 1877, and 5.24$\frac{3}{5}$ in 1879. Yet for the next ten years Cuyler and Harmer of Yale,

Morison of Harvard, and Faries of Pennsylvania, all averaged around 4.40, and in 1889 C. O. Wells of Amherst made the very excellent time of 4.29⅘. Then came the days of Jarvis, Orton, and Cregan. Jarvis won in 1893, 1894 and 1896, and his best time was 4.26⅕. Cregan won from 1898 to 1900, and made a record of 4.23⅗. Orton's name I have reserved until the last since he deserves a special paragraph by himself.

Although he won the intercollegiate mile in 1895 and 1897, like Wefers, Burke, Long, Kilpatrick and others, he was even more renowned for his work outside of college competition. He won championships innumerable, incidentally winning the national championship at the mile six times, and duplicating the feat in the two-mile steeplechase. He was a most consistent runner, always to be depended upon, and a most scientific student of the whole art and theory of distance and cross-country work.

After this trio, D. C. Munson of Cornell won the mile in 1904 and 1905, in the good time of 4.25⅗ and 4.25⅕. Then Haskins of Pennsylvania won for two years, in 1907 making his great record of 4.20⅗, which was expected to stand for years, but in 1909 Paull of Pennsylvania astonished every one by lowering Haskins's figures to $4.17\frac{4}{5}$, a performance which has set all followers of athletics wondering what may be expected from this new star before he has completed his college course, although in 1910, as noted above, he did not show the form of the preceding year and was beaten by P. J. Taylor of Cornell, in $4.23\frac{3}{5}$.

The two-mile run was not added to the intercollegiate programme until 1899. Alec Grant was the winner, and the year following made a record of $9.51\frac{3}{5}$, which stood for three years, when Schutt of Cornell lowered this time to 9.40. Again in 1907, Rowe of Michigan reduced the record to $9.34\frac{4}{5}$, and in 1909, Taylor of Cornell set the record which stands to-day, $9.27\frac{3}{5}$.

CHAPTER IV

COLLEGE DAYS — HEROES PAST AND PRESENT — THE HURDLERS, JUMPERS, AND WEIGHT-THROWERS

In no other event has the development in form, with its corresponding improvement in time, been more marked than in the hurdles. The low hurdles were not added to the intercollegiate programme until 1888, but in the high hurdles, during the first ten years 18 seconds was bettered only twice. W. H. Ludington of Yale, who won the event for three years in succession, was the first to make an even 17 seconds, and H. Mapes of Columbia, who succeeded him, brought this down to 16⅘. The first great name, however, is that of H. L. Williams of Yale, who in 1890 ran in 16⅕, and the year following improved his own record to 15⅘. After him came Harding of Columbia, and Cady and Perkins of Yale, all sixteen-second men, while in 1895, Stephen Chase of Dartmouth equaled the record of 15⅘. Chase was easily the leading hurdler of his time. He won the national championship in 1894 and 1895, and defeated Godfrey Shaw, the famous English hurdler, in the international games of the latter year.

The year 1898 marked the sensational appearance, already referred to in the preceding chapter, of Alvin C. Kraenzlein. His winning time in 1898 was 15$\frac{4}{5}$, and in the two following years he bettered this, on both occasions, by a fifth of a second. Kraenzlein did not confine his activities wholly to intercollegiate sport, and in 1898 won the national championship in the high and low hurdles, and the following year bettered this by winning four firsts, the hundred, the broad jump, and both hurdles; while in the Olympic games, at Paris, in 1900, he rounded out his career by winning the sixty yards, the high hurdles, and the broad jump.

After Kraenzlein's retirement the time in the high hurdles continued to be uniformly good. In the next eight or nine years, Clapp of Yale, Converse of Harvard, Amsler of Pennsylvania, Hubbard of Amherst, and Shaw of Dartmouth, all won in turn, and always in time better than 16 flat. Shaw was the best of the lot, but in 1907 his colors were lowered by one of the really great athletes of the age, J. C. Garrels of Michigan, who defeated him in the finals in the splendid time of $15\frac{1}{5}$.

At this same meeting Garrels won the low hurdles in 24 seconds, and was second in the shot. It is hard to imagine a more ideally built man for a great athlete. A giant in stature, and yet with the speed to run the hurdles in such splendid time — it is a combination not met with once in a thousand times. And yet, strangely enough, even two such hurdlers as Garrels and Shaw — both with records of $15\frac{1}{5}$ seconds — were destined to go down to defeat before Forrest C. Smithson, the Western hurdler, in the finals of the Olympic games at London, in 1908. Such a field — Garrels, Shaw, Smithson, and Rand of Harvard — never before faced a starter in a high-hurdle race. Smithson won in 15 seconds flat, — a new world's record, — with Garrels second and Shaw third. A race to go down in history famous for all time.

To return to Garrels himself. I have been asked over and over again whether I believe Garrels could defeat Martin Sheridan in an all-around competition. It is a question like the famous, "Have you stopped beating your wife yet?" which can hardly be answered by a di-

JOHN GARRELS

rect yes or no. I should attempt to give an answer in this way. First of all, I believe Garrels to be the greater natural athlete of the two; and I say this advisedly, realizing to the full, as one who has met defeat at his hands, what a wonder Sheridan is. Garrels is the larger man, Sheridan's equal in spring, and his superior in speed and strength. Therefore, by nature, he should be the better performer of the two. So much for theory; but when we come to face actual ability, as the men rank at the present moment, no one who has not tried it can realize the length of the preparation which is necessary to fit a man to compete in first-class company in the all-arounds.

Sheridan did not blossom forth as a wonder all in a' season. He served a long and arduous apprenticeship before he could make the consistent showing that he does to-day at each one of the ten different events. We know what he can do; with Garrels, in many of the events it is largely conjecture. To begin with the weights, we know that Garrels is the better man in the shot; and it seems almost certain that, with the proper coaching, he should be a wonderful performer with both the hammer and the fifty-six, — fully as good as, if not better than, Sheridan.

In the high hurdles Garrels, of course, would again be far ahead, and he should win in the hundred as well. The half-mile walk and the mile run would probably be events at which Sheridan would make the better showing — the first, because the knack is not learned in a day; the second, because a man as large as Garrels does not usually take kindly to the strain of the mile. Still, there are exceptions, and with Garrels's football experience and his immense strength, I do not see why the mile should trouble him. In the high jump, and the broad, the men should be about equal, while the pole-vault would be, in all probability, Garrels's weakest point, as it is one of Sheridan's strongest. On the whole, while the entire matter is problematical, and will, I fear, never become an actuality, I should be of opinion, that given a year or two to devote to preparation for the games, Garrels should win. This, however, as I say, is conjecture only, — merely a personal opinion, — and however much we may theorize, we *know* what Sheridan can do, because he has left the figures, in black and white, behind him.

To return, after this digression, to the hurdlers. The low hurdles were added to the intercollegiate programme in 1888, and thus, even from the start, we find the time of the winners always respectable, and for the most part remarkably good. Most of the fast low hurdlers have been equally good over the high, but there have been noteworthy exceptions. Thus, while Mapes of Columbia, Williams, Perkins, Clapp, and Howe of Yale, Kraenzlein of Pennsylvania, Willis of Harvard, Hubbard of Amherst, Castleman of Colgate, and Garrels of Michigan, were all first-class performers, over both the high and the low, on the other hand, Lee, Fearing, and Bremer of Harvard, and Sheldon of Yale, while among the best at the low, never made any showing at the high.

J. P. Lee of Harvard, famous on the football field, and possessing great speed at the shorter distances, won the race in 1890, and held the record of 24⅘ until J. L. Bremer of Harvard lowered this by a fifth of a second. Bremer won in 1894, 1895, and 1896, and met his first defeat, already referred to, in 1898, when Kraenzlein made his phenomenal record of 23⅗. In 1902, J. G. Willis of Harvard made the next best time to Kraenzlein, 23⅘. Willis was an athlete whose name is not so widely known as it should be, simply for the reason that he confined himself to college competition. He was one of the strongest hurdlers I have ever seen —very fast at the high, as well,—but the longer distance suited him to perfection. The further he ran, the better he seemed to like it, and I do not think, in the athletic world at large, he has ever quite gained the standing he deserves for this remarkable race. When one considers that the great Garrels, in 1907, ran his race in 24 seconds flat, and that this was $\frac{3}{5}$ of a second faster than any other intercollegiate winner except Kraenzlein, then one can realize what Willis's time really means. In 1899 Howe of Yale won both hurdles, the high in 15$\frac{3}{5}$, and the low in 24$\frac{4}{5}$, two fine performances; and in 1910 Gardner of Harvard won the low hurdles in 24$\frac{3}{5}$.

The one-mile walk has been discarded from the programme now for ten years, and was, I think, wisely given up. The great difficulty of telling whether a man is running or not, the bad feeling almost invariably arising out of the ruling off of those who the judges think are not walking fair "heel and toe," — all of this was disagreeable and a sure cause of trouble.

The three famous names on the list of winners are Borcherling of Princeton, Thrall of

Yale, and Fetterman of Pennsylvania. Borcherling, in 1892, was the first man to beat
seven minutes. He won his race in 6.52$\frac{4}{5}$, and
this record stood for a half-dozen years, although Thrall of Yale walked in 6.54$\frac{4}{5}$ in 1896.
Finally, in 1898, the last year in which the
event was held, Fetterman established the
record of 6.45$\frac{4}{5}$, which for obvious reasons still
stands to-day.

In looking over the list of winners in the running broad jump, at the intercollegiates, any
one who is interested in athletics can hardly
fail to be struck by one fact about the event,
and that is, that the broad jump combines
more readily with an athlete's other specialties than does any other contest on the programme. Apart from the professed all-around
men, a man is usually either a sprinter, or a
middle-distance man, or a miler, or a hurdler,
or a jumper, or a weight man. But in the broad
jump, since it depends partly upon speed and
partly upon spring, we find all kinds of interesting combinations. One man wins the sprints
and the broad jump, another the high jump
and the broad jump, another the pole vault and
the broad jump, another the hurdles and the
broad jump, and, most curious of all, one

athlete actually makes a double win of the broad jump and the half-mile.

The most common case is that of the man who is a good sprinter and a good broad jumper as well. In fact, speed is such an essential part of the broad jump that any good hundred-yards man, with very little preparation, is practically sure of being able to get out and clear twenty feet. In the second year of the intercollegiates, 1877, we find a triple winner in H. H. Lee of Pennsylvania who won the hundred, two-twenty, and broad jump, covering, in the last-named event, the very fair distance of 19 feet and 7 inches. For the next two years, 1878 and 1879, the winner was J. P. Conover of Columbia. Conover was another of the double winners already referred to, for in both of these years he won the high jump as well, and in the latter year cleared 5 feet $8\frac{1}{4}$ inches in the high, and an even 20 feet in the broad.

In 1881, J. F. Jenkins, Jr. of Columbia improved the record to 20 feet $9\frac{1}{4}$, which stood for three years, until in 1884, O. Bodelson, also of Columbia, made a distance of 21 feet $3\frac{1}{2}$.

In the previous year, 1883, occurs the name of a man who was a remarkably good all-around jumper. This was W. Soren of Harvard, who won the event that year with a jump of 20 feet and 6 inches. In 1880 Soren had been the winner in the standing high and standing broad jumps; the next year he won the standing high and the running high; and he won the latter event again in 1882, and the pole-vault as well.

In 1887 appears the first really great name among the intercollegiate broad jumpers, T. G. Shearman, Jr., of Yale. He won for three years in succession, and in 1888 won the pole-vault besides. But it is as a broad jumper that he has made his fame secure, for his records for the three years were 21 feet and 11 inches, 20 feet and 8 inches, and, last and best, 22 feet and 6 inches.

From this time on seldom do the records fall below 22 feet. The next year, 1890, W. C. Dohm of Princeton, the famous middle-distance man, performed the remarkable feat of capturing the half-mile in $1.57\frac{1}{5}$ and winning the broad jump with a leap of 22 feet $3\frac{1}{2}$ inches. The succeeding year witnessed the breaking of the record, Victor Mapes of Columbia coming within three quarters of an inch of the even 23 feet. Then came the day of E. B. Bloss of Harvard, who won in 1892 and 1893, in the latter year with the fine jump of 22 feet $9\frac{5}{8}$. Bloss was a wonderful athlete, seeming at first sight little more than a midget in size, but once stripped down to athletic costume, revealing muscles of tremendous power, and appearing in action a compact, flying ball of sheer nervous energy. At the short dashes he was unbeatable; he was a champion at the broad jump and the hop, step, and jump, a good high jumper, and a fair hurdler; altogether a remarkable man.

In 1894 E. S. Ramsdell of Pennsylvania equaled the feat of H. H. Lee, accomplished almost twenty years before, by winning both dashes and the broad jump, clearing 22 feet 1 inch in the broad. In 1895 and 1896 L. P. Sheldon of Yale was the winner, with 22 feet 8½, and 22 feet 3¼ for the two years. Many were the battles between Sheldon and Bloss, first one winning, then the other, and the contrast between them never failed to arouse the interest of the crowd. Sheldon was just about a foot higher than Bloss, and to watch the latter tearing down at the take-off, with all his tremendous speed, and then to watch Sheldon's mighty strides, seeming really slow and deliberate in comparison, revealed a difference in method and in physical make-up too striking ever to be forgotten. Sheldon, like his rival, was a most versatile athlete, and a winner of the national all-around championship in 1896. The broad jump was his specialty, but he could perform with better than average ability at almost every event on the programme.

In 1897 Remington of Pennsylvania was the winner, and then came the days of Prinstein and Kraenzlein, — a meeting of two veritable champions. I have heard the question discussed again and again as to which was really the better broad jumper. I myself should not care to answer it. Prinstein was the intercollegiate champion in 1898 and 1900, winning with jumps of 23 feet $7\frac{3}{8}$ and 23 feet 8. Kraenzlein was the champion in 1899, when he established the intercollegiate record of 24 feet $4\frac{1}{4}$. Prinstein holds the American record of 24 feet $7\frac{1}{4}$, and won the Olympic championship at St. Louis, in 1904, with 24 feet and 1 inch, and again at Athens, in 1906, with 23 feet $7\frac{1}{2}$. Kraenzlein was Olympic champion at Paris, in 1900, winning with 23 feet $6\frac{7}{8}$. Two great jumpers, — so great that there seems little to be gained in an attempt to rank one of them above the other.

After Prinstein's last win, in 1900, there was a dearth of similar records until 1904, when

Stangland of Columbia cleared 23 feet 6½. The next year also saw a fine performance when Simons of Princeton made 23 feet 2½, and in 1906 and 1907 Knox of Yale maintained the standard with winning jumps of 23 feet 4½ and 22 feet 10. In 1908 Cook of Cornell won with 22 feet 8, and in 1909 repeated his win with a jump of 22 feet 6¼. In 1910, Roberts of Amherst won with a jump of 22 feet 7¼.

Thus the list of the college broad jumpers reveals a group of notable performers; and in the companion event, the running high jump, the story is the same. Conover of Columbia, who won the high and the broad jumps in both 1877 and 1878, has already been spoken of, and so has Soren of Harvard, who won in 1881 and 1882. In 1883 and 1884 C. H. Atkinson, also of Harvard, won with the good jumps of 5 feet 8½ and 5 feet 9¾.

In the next year, 1885, appears the famous name of W. Byrd Page, Jr., of Pennsylvania. Page not only won the intercollegiates for three years in succession, but, as every one knows, accomplished the feat of jumping 6 feet and 4 inches, which still stands as the collegiate record, and with the single exception of M. F. Sweeney's still more wonderful performance,

MICHAEL F. SWEENEY

has stood the test of time, unchallenged in open competition, for five-and-twenty years.

Page passed along his title to a fellow Pennsylvanian, I. D. Webster, who won for two years in succession, and then comes the name of that famous Harvard athlete, G. R. Fearing, Jr., who succeeded in doing in the high jump what Sherrill of Yale had already accomplished in the hundred yards — winning for four consecutive years, with the fine records of 5 feet 8½, 6 feet, 6 feet ½ inch, and 5 feet 10¾. In 1892 Fearing showed his versatility by winning the low hurdles as well, in the good time of 25⅗.

After Fearing, Paine of Harvard and Leslie of Pennsylvania each held the title for a year, and then came another famous performer, J. D. Winsor, Jr., of Pennsylvania, who won in 1896 and 1897, and tied for first in 1898. In 1897 Winsor made his best record, 6 feet 3, a jump only once exceeded in the whole list of intercollegiate meetings.

From Winsor's time on, great jumpers have been plenty. In 1899 I. K. Baxter of Pennsylvania won with 6 feet 2. Baxter, besides being a college champion, was much more widely known as a competitor in the colors of the

New York Athletic Club. He was four times national champion in the high jump, won the pole-vault in 1889, with 10 feet and 9 inches, and was Olympic champion, at Paris, in 1900, with a jump of 6 feet $2\frac{1}{4}$.

The next winner had a record almost identical with Baxter's. This was S. S. Jones of New York University. He won the intercollegiates in 1900 and 1901; he also competed for the New York Athletic Club, was three times national champion, once with a jump of 6 feet 2, and was Olympic champion, at St. Louis, in 1904.

Even after these great athletes, three other famous names still remain on the lists. The first of these is that of R. P. Kernan, of Harvard, one of the finest natural athletes who ever stepped. Kernan was another man of the type of Fearing, one who could do anything in athletics that he chose to turn his hand to, and could do it, in addition, surpassingly well. Half-back on the eleven, catcher on the nine, and then, like his almost equally great predecessor, C. J. Paine, Jr., ready to step coolly out on the track, in time of need, and without practice, casually to win the Yale games with a jump of 6 feet, and the intercollegiates with a jump of 6 feet 1. Before ability such as Kernan's we ordinary mortals can only shrug our shoulders, and in the slang of the day, murmur disgustedly, "Oh, what's the use?"

To Kernan succeeded Marshall of Yale, who won in 1905 and 1906, and in 1907 had his great duel, at the Harvard Stadium, with Moffit of Pennsylvania, when Moffit won, and had to break the intercollegiate record to do it, clearing 6 feet 3¼, while Marshall finished second, with 6 feet 2.

Page, Fearing, Winsor, Baxter, Jones, Kernan, Marshall, Moffit, — search a long time before you will come again upon such a list of jumpers; all good at record-making, and all sterling contestants as well, doing their best when their best was needed, and forming a group to challenge comparison with the world.

From the lithe and active men who have become famous through their skill in jumping, it is a far cry to the sturdy giants who have been winners with the weights — the 16-pound shot and the 16-pound hammer. Since, in the weights, once given the knack of the event, strength and size may be counted upon as aids to success with an almost mathematical precision, — since, in the sporting phrase, in the hammer and shot, "a good big 'un will always beat a good little 'un," these events find an' added interest from the fact that among the winners are found many of the men who have made their fame secure, in line or backfield, on the "gridiron."

In the shot-put, almost at the very beginning of the list, we come upon the name of F. Larkin of Princeton, who found in the intercollegiates a fertile field for his all-around abilities. He won the shot in 1877, and in 1878 and 1879 won no less than four events in each year — the shot, the hammer, the standing high jump, and the standing broad. His best record with the shot was 33 feet $8\frac{1}{2}$, made in 1879.

After Larkin came another three-year winner, A. T. Moore of Stevens, who improved upon Larkin's figures, and in 1882 made his best record of 36 feet 3. And then, in 1886 and 1887, we come upon the name of A. B. Coxe of Yale, even more famous as a hammer-thrower, but a giant with the shot as well, making winning puts, first of 38 feet $9\frac{1}{2}$, and then of 40 feet $9\frac{1}{2}$.

After Coxe, came Pennypacker of Harvard, then the mighty Janeway of Princeton, then Finlay and Evins of Harvard, and then one who made his name famous for all time: football player, shot-putter, hammer-thrower, — a champion at all three, — W. O. Hickok of Yale. Hickok won the shot in 1893, 1894, and 1895, with puts of 41 feet $\frac{1}{2}$ inch, 42 feet flat, and 42 feet $11\frac{1}{2}$.

I shall never forget the impression that Hickok's physique made upon me when he came to Cambridge to take part in the dual games on Holmes Field. There have been champions who did not look the part; there have been champions who you felt might somehow be defeated; but Hickok was none of these. His reputation was something tremendous; even his name in print used to make shivers run up and down our backs, as we saw those five points in the shot and the five more in the hammer already on their way to New Haven. I do not know whether Hickok himself quite realized his fame. I doubt it. Most of the great athletes I have known have been exceptionally modest men. And Hickok seemed to take his athletic diversions lightly, almost boyishly, not with the strained seriousness that has characterized so many champions. The call for his event would be given; he would come jogging across the field, his favorite shot, slung in a towel, in his hand. His name would be called; he would step into the circle, poise easily for a moment, without apparent exertion—and then, a short hop, a quick turn of his body, and the contest was over. Somewhere between 41 and 44 feet, — it did n't particularly matter where; the five points were gone, and we could only say, turning our faces toward the future, "Well, some day he 's got to graduate, anyway." It was a cheering thought.

Hickok had a worthy successor in "Dick" Sheldon, brother of L. P. Sheldon, of broad-jump and all-around fame. Sheldon won in 1896, and again in 1901, in the latter year with the good put of 43 feet $9\frac{1}{4}$. In 1898 and 1899 J. C. McCracken, the famous Pennsylvania football player, was the winner, with 43 feet $8\frac{1}{2}$ and 42 feet $\frac{1}{2}$ inch. McCracken was about as healthy and sturdy a specimen as I have ever beheld; he was an enthusiastic athlete, went into things with a will, and "got results" in a most unquestioned manner.

After McCracken, Beck of Yale won the event three times, in 1900, 1902, and 1903. 44 feet 3 inches; 44 feet $8\frac{1}{2}$ inches; and 46 feet flat; those were his winning puts, and the last of them remained as the intercollegiate record

until W. F. Krueger of Swarthmore, succeeding
to Schoenfuss and Stephenson of Harvard, and
Porter of Cornell, established, in 1907, the present record of 46 feet 5¼. Krueger won again
in 1908, and in 1909 C. C. Little of Harvard, a
man who has improved steadily all through his
shot-putting career, made his best record by
winning with a put of 46 feet 2, defeating
Krueger by nearly a foot. In 1910 Horner of
Michigan won with a put of 46 feet 4½.

In the hammer-throw, there are two interesting things to be noted at the outset. The
first is that some men are good performers,
both with the shot and with the hammer, while
others, though gaining a thorough mastery over
one of the events, fail utterly in the companion
contest. The two events, indeed, are entirely
dissimilar in principle: one is a push, the other
a pull; and the man who excels at both can
never be accused of being entirely lacking in
"athletic brains." Thus we find Coxe and
Hickok of Yale, Finlay and Evins of Harvard,
Woodruff and McCracken of Pennsylvania, all
double winners with both shot and hammer,
while Sheldon, Beck, Schoenfuss, Stephenson,
and Krueger all distinguished themselves with
the shot alone, and on the other hand, men

like Chadwick of Yale, Plaw of California, and De Witt of Princeton, achieved their greatest success with the hammer alone.

Another thing of interest about the hammer throw is the evolution, both of the hammer itself and of the manner of throwing it. In the old days the hammer was an iron ball, with a stiff wooden handle, and was thrown from a stand. Then the rules were changed so as to permit the athlete to throw within a seven-foot circle, turning his body around to gain additional momentum. After this the head of the hammer was changed from iron to lead, and the handle was changed to the thinnest of wires, with a double grip, in shape like a stirrup, instead of the straight handle of old days. Finally, with the appearance of John Flanagan, the double turn succeeded to the single, and then the triple to the double, so that with all these changes and improvements the records of the early days have been more than doubled by the skilled performers of the present.

The first great intercollegiate hammer-thrower was A. B. Coxe of Yale, already mentioned as a winning shot-putter as well. He achieved the same distinction in the hammer that Sherrill had gained in the hundred, and

Fearing in the high jump, winning for four years in succession, with records constantly improving from 83 feet 2, to 98 feet 6.

In 1891, Finlay of Harvard threw 107 feet $7\frac{1}{2}$ inches, and this remained as the record until the appearance, two years later, of Hickok of Yale. Hickok threw 110 feet $4\frac{1}{2}$ inches, in 1893, and then occurred the change in the rules by which the contestants were allowed to throw with a turn. As a result, the records began immediately to show improvement. In 1894 Hickok threw 123 feet 9 inches, and the following year increased his distance to 135 feet $7\frac{1}{2}$. Then came Chadwick of Yale, who won with 132 feet $6\frac{1}{2}$, and then Woodruff of Pennsylvania, who bettered Hickok's record with a throw of 136 feet 3.

No hammer record was long safe, however, in these days, for now came the introduction of the double turn, and the next year McCracken of Pennsylvania threw 149 feet, 5 inches, and won again the year following with 144 feet 1 inch.

In 1900, Plaw of California raised the record again to 154 feet $4\frac{1}{2}$; and then came the day of the man who was to share with Sherrill, Fearing, and Coxe the honor of being a four-time winner, — J. R. De Witt of Princeton. De Witt won from 1901 to 1904 inclusive; in 1902 he made the intercollegiate record of 164 feet 10 inches, which stands to-day, and also established the collegiate record of 166 feet 5. A giant in strength, and a master of the art of the double turn—surely a combination hard to beat. Talbot of Cornell won in 1909, with 158 feet 9$\frac{1}{2}$, and Cooney of Yale in 1910, with 152 feet 5.

In the pole-vault the improvement has been nearly as marked as in the hammer-throw. The whole method of performing the event was revolutionized with the change in the grip of the hands — the lower hand sliding up until the two pulled at the same time practically as one. Starting in the first year of the intercollegiates with a record of 7 feet 4, by Pryor of Columbia, Toler of Princeton was the first man to reach 10 feet, in 1883, and Stevens of Columbia the first man to exceed it, three years later, with a vault of 10 feet 3$\frac{1}{4}$. Leavitt of Harvard and Ryder of Yale in turn improved upon these figures, and in 1895 Buchholz of Pennsylvania cleared the great height, for those days, of 11 feet 3$\frac{3}{4}$. In 1898, Clapp of Yale and Hoyt of Harvard tied at 11 feet 4$\frac{1}{4}$, and a year later Clapp cleared 11 feet 5.

WALTER R. DRAY

This record stood until 1902, when Horton of Princeton did 11 feet 7, figures exactly equaled the year following by Gardner of Syracuse, and improved to 11 feet $8\frac{3}{4}$ in 1904, by McLanahan of Yale.

In recent years, Dray and Gilbert of Yale, and Cook of Cornell, have been three famous vaulters, while in 1909 Campbell of Yale made a new intercollegiate record of 12 feet $3\frac{1}{4}$, and in 1910 Nelson of Yale raised the figures to 12 feet $4\frac{3}{8}$.

CHAPTER V

THE ALL-AROUND CHAMPIONSHIP

IT was from James E. Morse, in 1893, that I first heard of the all-around championship. Morse had little sympathy with the athlete who clings to one specialty, and he himself, practising as he preached, had tried every event on the athletic calendar. At the time when I knew him, however, his athletic career was practically ended, and though a fine performer for his weight and size, he was never of that rugged build which best meets the demands of all-around competition. Yet though his days of active work were over, his interest was still as keen as ever, and seeing in me, I think, a possible champion in embryo, he made haste to acquaint me with the history of the all-arounds.

I shall never forget my feelings as I listened to his description of the games. They attracted me, in the first place, by their very difficulty. Those adventurers who seek to discover either pole, almost invariably, if they do not perish in their search, return again and again to their quest. They have encountered hardship, danger, suffering; their sober judgment bids them cease; yet imagination conquers in the end, and the lure of the frozen ice-fields calls to them over many a league of roaring sea. And thus, in lesser degree, the all-arounds were my temptation. Truly, the outlook was staggering; the prospect of success seemed infinitely small. For I learned that, first of all, the contestants must run a hundred yards on time, and that this was followed by the putting of the shot, and by the high jump. So far, so good; but next on the programme came the half-mile walk, and the science of heel-and-toe walking, as I then suspected, and later was to know to my cost, is not a thing (excepting on the part of the spectators) to be treated with levity. Then followed, in quick succession, the hammer-throw, the pole-vault, the hurdle race, the broad jump, the throwing of the fifty-six-pound weight, and last of all (I was infinitely relieved to find that there *was* a last) the mile run. Here was a test, indeed, in the face of which my poor list of accomplishments seemed pitifully inadequate. For while I was a high jumper of perhaps a little less than average ability, and while I had shown some aptitude for sprinting, there my knowledge ceased. Of the other eight events I knew nothing at all. I had but a casual nodding acquaintance with a hammer, and a fifty-six-pound weight I had never seen. To balance the scale I had only youth, some physical qualifications for the task, and above all, the blessed optimism of inexperience. Altogether, the attempt seemed little short of herculean.

Besides the difficulties it presented, one other feature of the all-arounds attracted me. This was the method of scoring, for the games were not a contest, in the accepted meaning of the word, but resembled rather a species of athletic examination paper, each man, whether he won or lost, being marked for his performance, in each event, on a graded scale. Ten thousand points was the possible maximum, based on the possibility of a man's equaling the world's record in each of the ten events. Thus, a man who ran the hundred yards in record time would be credited with a thousand points, while at the other end of the scale there would be an arbitrary minimum, corresponding to a performance so poor that a boy of ten might have equaled it. And for every fraction of a second between these two extremes, there would be a gain or loss of so many points. There was a definiteness, a mathematical exactness, in this method of measuring one's ability, which impressed me greatly, even though in the majority of the events I could see the empty zeros staring me in the face. There appears to be a feeling curiously akin to self-contentment in being at the very foot of the ladder. "At least," we say, "this cannot well be worse. We are on the ground, and barring earthquakes, we cannot go much lower. And perhaps, little by little, a rung at a time, we may some day go climbing the ladder after all."

Besides these two reasons, there was a third, more important still — the associations which even the name of the event calls to mind, the glamour of the list of famous athletes to be found from the very beginning on its rolls. In the first year in which the championships were held the winner was W. R. Thompson of Montreal, while second and third to him were Malcolm W. Ford and A. A. Jordan, than whose no two names, perhaps, have ever been more famous in our athletic history. Of the three men, I was destined to meet Thompson twelve years later, in Montreal. I had gone there to compete in the Canadian championships, had taken part in five events, and won three seconds and a third. Coming home in the car from the grounds, a gentleman leaned across the aisle and said to me: "My name is Thompson. I was watching your work this afternoon, and I think some day you ought to try the all-arounds. It seems to me you would have a chance to win." To some people in the world, the simple introduction, "My name is Thompson," might not at once have revealed the owner's identity; but to me there was but one Thompson in the world, and all the rest of the way back to the hotel I kept stealing covert glances at the man who had been a champion in his day, and who had triumphed over Ford and Jordan. After this, Ford was to win the title four times, and Jordan three, so that up to 1895 these two giants of athletics kept the championship well guarded, and the names of M. O'Sullivan and E. W. Goff are the only others to be bracketed with theirs. Jordan I saw in actual competition; Ford I met in 1897; and I had some correspondence with him later over an article which he was preparing on the measurements of all-around athletes.

Thus the time had come when I must make my start; for no one, I suppose, has ever yet be-

MALCOLM W. FORD

come an athlete merely by sitting still and thinking about it. Not that I would be misunderstood. Thought is of inestimable value in all kinds of active sport; but thought alone is not enough. There must be added the rough-and-ready stimulant of real exercise. Theory is invaluable, but it must have practical experience to build upon. "There must be bloody noses and cracked crowns," — always figuratively, sometimes literally as well. And thus I plunged headforemost into the business of learning — or trying to learn — the theory and the practice of athletic sports.

What I went through I can best illustrate by an experience from another branch of life. I have a friend who owned one of the first small motor-boats in use in Massachusetts Bay. He learned to run her in the cold, hard school of practical endeavor, to the accompaniment of aching back and blistered palms. And yet experience, though a hard teacher, is a thorough one as well, and behold, as the years passed, my friend waxed great in knowledge, until to-day, lacking the title, he is a very professor of motor-boats. There is not a refractory engine in the town in which he lives — nay, I doubt if one exists throughout the state — which must not, soon or late, yield to the magic of his touch, and whir away as merrily and smoothly as the best. And yet, when the other day I paid him a compliment upon his knowledge, he only shook his head. "Something of what you say," he replied, "is true. But if I could have looked ahead — if I could have foreseen the damage I should do to body and mind, and I fear to my immortal soul besides, I should have known the day I bought that engine to be the most tragic of my entire life. And if I could have looked ahead through the long, weary years, the day after I bought the engine I should have gone out and bought an axe."

And thus, to anticipate a little, my experience in athletics was to be somewhat like that of my unhappy friend. If I could have cast a prophetic glance forward through the years, and have seen myself, in dim perspective, learning to pole-vault, learning to hurdle, learning to throw the hammer, learning to walk (I seem, unconsciously, to be paraphrasing the titles of the "Rollo" books), I am sure that at the sight I should have abandoned the struggle. My very blood would have curdled, and the fires of enthusiasm have been frozen in my veins. But the veil of the future, mercifully enough, is spread before us. I could not foresee what an inapt pupil I was to prove; and so, with the all-sufficing ignorance of youth, set hopefully enough to work upon my task.

It was not all hard work. With that part of the programme which comprised the jumps, I had no stupendous difficulty. I could high-jump reasonably well already; the broad jump was one of the few events which seemed to come to me, as it were, by nature; and thus there was only the pole-vault left. And to all beginners, who may be tempted to despair by the ignoble qualities of a first performance, let me confess, not without a blush of shame, the actual height which I cleared in my first effort at the vault — 4 feet and 9 inches! No more, no less. And this is no flight of fancy, but actual fact; while at this very time, moreover, in an ordinary running jump, I could clear in the vicinity of $5\frac{1}{2}$ feet. The reason was not far to seek. I had not learned to trust my full weight to the pole, or to pull upwards with my arms. In consequence, the pole, instead of becoming a help, served merely to encumber me, and in the manner in which I made use of it, was worse for me than no aid at all. Gradually, however, I mastered the theory of the vault, and while I never became more than a very ordinary performer, was still able to make a showing not altogether bad.

With the running events, there were more troubles to be faced. I had no great difficulty with the dash; like the broad jump, it seemed to come to me naturally. The mile run I detested, — not so much, I think, on account of the actual effort involved, as for the dreary monotony of circling round and round the track, at the same steady jog. It failed to inspire me, I was loth to practise it, and as a result, my performance in competition was extremely bad. The hurdle race troubled me for a time, until I learned the lesson, easy to say and hard to put in practice, that the race was not a combination of running and jumping, but a running event, pure and simple, with the hurdles merely so many obstacles, to be cleared in one's stride. Once having mastered this idea, the rest was easy. Once or twice, indeed, I fell heavily, and filled my knees with cinders, but on the whole I showed, comparatively speaking, quite an aptitude for the event, and learned to run the distance at what, for those days, was a very respectable speed.

But with the half-mile walk, my varied experiences were little short of ludicrous. To the uninitiated, the walking of a half-mile seems a simple thing; but, alas, the "walk" of athletics is not the simple thing of daily life. On the contrary, it is a deliberate contortion of the body with which Heaven has furnished us; a grotesque parade of writhing hips, agonized face and brandished arms; a spectacle at which the lookers-on are moved to violent laughter, and the performers themselves are affected to the verge of tears. I shall long remember my faithful practice at the old Irvington Street Oval. Round and round the little track I toiled, while various small boys reclined at ease upon the grass outside, and cheered me with friendly encouragement and criticism. "Go it, old feller! You're doin' fine!" "Ah, he's runnin'!" "Keep it up, ol' ice-wagon!" These were a few of the less insulting comments, and it took all my determination to persevere in the face of them. Even the old-time professional whom I finally engaged to coach me was unflatteringly free with his judgment upon my style. He would stand and watch me, as I circled the track, my eyes fixed hopefully upon his face, to see if I might read any encouragement there. Alas! I never did. He would shake his head impatiently. "You don't walk natural," he would object; and, indeed, I felt my only crumb of comfort to be in the thought that if I were walking "natural," I should be in a very bad way indeed. A week later, hoping vainly for a word of praise, I asked him if he could not see some improvement. He gazed at me with contracted brows. "Like to enter you at a cake-walk," he grimly responded; "we'd get a prize there, anyway"; and with that I must be content. But my crowning humiliation was still to come, and though I should not disturb the chronology of my efforts by telling of it here, it is a story that I am always glad to have out of the way.

It was two years later that I competed for the national all-around championship for the first time. All went well until the half-mile walk was reached. There were nine starters, and I had a dismal foreboding, as I toed the scratch, concerning the position I should occupy at the conclusion of the race. I was entirely correct in my surmise. The other eight contestants had all finished when I came toiling up the stretch, weary, hot, exhausted, and with the painful consciousness that I was making an egregious fool of myself. As I passed the crowded grand-stand, a little girl leaned forward from the front row, and in her childish treble, piped] out, with a certain delighted wonder in her tone, "Oh, mother, just look at this one coming!" There was a delighted roar from the grand-stand, and my cheeks, as I toiled on, flushed even redder than before.

Nor were difficulties lacking in the weight events. The knack of the shot-put I acquired gradually, and since the principle of throwing the fifty-six-pound weight is fundamentally the same as that of the hammer-throw, once successful with the latter, I had no trouble with the heavier missile. But the hammer itself! Words alone are inadequate to tell of my trials. My first attempt to throw it was in my Freshman year in college. I picked it up on Holmes Field, and guilelessly asked a friend to give me some idea of the knack of throwing it. He told me that the two essentials were to swing it rapidly, and at a considerable height from the ground. I prefer to think he was merely ignorant. However that may have been, the advice was like the famous coaching of Mr. Verdant Green, "Dip your oar in deep, and bring it out with a jerk." I braced my feet, and swung manfully, and when the hammer was going at what seemed to me lightning speed, essayed to turn.

The result was little short of volcanic. I can only describe what occurred from the testimony of disinterested bystanders. They said that I dove headlong through space, like a man attempting to fly. One classmate, with a taste for rhetoric, wrote a daily theme on the occurrence, under the caption, "The greatest acrobatic feat of modern times." I should have liked to witness the performance myself, but that is a privilege denied to the protagonist. In any event, even if they exaggerated a trifle in other particulars, I am sure they spoke only the truth when they told me that the first portion of my anatomy to reach the ground, after my brief ascension, was the back of my neck. I am confident of it. It was not merely conjecture. I had the proofs upon my person for a week.

At length I rose, and somewhat dizzily looked about me. Many a time since then I have seen some hapless golfer make a tremendous lunge at his ball, and misled by the force of his stroke, at first gaze hopefully away into the far distance; then, half doubtfully, nearer and nearer home; and finally, with a changing countenance pitiful to behold, look down at his feet to see the little ball still peacefully reposing there, untouched and unharmed. My experience was much the same. Something had been traveling at great speed; that I knew; and I supposed it to have been the hammer. I resembled the old lady who took her first ride on a railway train, and when the train ran off the track, was the only passenger who remained perfectly calm and unafraid. "I s'posed," she said afterwards, "that was the way the pesky thing always stopped." Thus I think that I at first accepted my somewhat muddled condition as one of the regular incidents of the hammer-throw. But when |I had gazed around the field, and then, as my vision gradually cleared, at last perceived the hammer, which had torn an ugly gash in the smooth green turf, lying only a few yards away; when I turned toward the "bleachers" and beheld the spectators there still doubled up and helpless with merriment, my injured feelings overcame me. I shall make no attempt here, with the aid of dots and dashes, to reproduce my remarks. They were sufficiently lurid, and I blush even to-day at recalling them. Youth is an intemperate season; and yet I think there was some shadow of excuse, after all.

The burned child dreads the fire, and for

weeks I could not look upon a hammer without a shudder. Yet a little later manlier feelings asserted themselves. I spent my summer vacations at the sea-shore where, among many other pleasant and delightful things, there was a long, level beach of smooth white sand. Surveying this one day, it struck me as an excellent battle-ground whereon to renew my contest with my enemy. The day after, I purchased a hammer. The day after that — I need not say how cautiously — I began my campaign. One eye I kept always on that hammer. I really think that I almost endowed it, in my mind, with life, as a kind of malignant devil, that might at any moment take me unawares, striking me in the back of the neck, or inserting itself between my feet, and hurling me prone to the earth. Yet gradually, with infinite patience and endeavor, I discovered that I was beginning to master the art. And one day, in a great illumination of understanding, I perceived the theory of the throw, and putting it into practice, achieved a distance beyond the Harvard record itself. I went around for the rest of that day in a kind of blissful daze, wondering if I could ever repeat that throw in actual competition, and vindicate myself for my first defeat.

JOHN FLANAGAN

October came at last, and with it the holding of the 'Varsity games, and my opportunity. My long practice had its reward, and with a throw of 123 feet and 7 inches, I shattered the College record by a dozen feet.

Such, in brief, were a few of my trials in preparing for the all-arounds. I have said, half-jestingly, that could I have looked ahead and foreseen them, I should never have ventured to persevere. But in reality I suppose that this is not true. "'T is not in mortals to command success"; but to make the effort — that is the common privilege of all. I was speaking the other day to a famous physician of the growing practice of a younger member of the profession. He nodded a little grimly. "It's all right," he said, "as long as it does'n't all come too easily. A man, in this world, ought to work for everything he gets." And while, from his point of view, the work was a means to an end, that end being success in the eye of the world, the most beautiful of modern writers has gone further still, believing that work, rightly done, *is* success, no matter how it may be judged by mortal eyes. Let us turn once more to "Virginibus Puerisque," and there read again: "O toiling hands of mortals! O unwearied feet, traveling you know not whither! Soon, soon, it seems to you, you must come forth on some conspicuous hill-top, and but a little way further, against the setting sun, descry the spires of El Dorado. Little do ye know your own blessedness; for to travel hopefully is a better thing than to arrive, and the true success is to labor."

In the summer of 1895 I entered my first all-around competition — the championship of New England. In a number of ways the contest was a noteworthy one. There were four competitors — L. A. (familiarly known as "Lenny") Carpenter of Wakefield, "Dan" Long and myself from the B. A. A., and F. H. Brigham of Worcester. In size and build we varied about as widely as four men in an all-around championship well could. Carpenter, at one extreme of the scale, was one of the few small men who ever contrived to make a success of such a programme. I do not think he weighed over a hundred and forty-five at the outside, yet he was experienced, cool-headed, and resourceful, possessing the temperament which excels in active competition. The weights would naturally have been his weakest point, yet he had made such a careful study of athletics that his excellence in form made up in great measure for his deficiency in power; he performed fairly well with the hammer and fifty-six, and in the shot achieved a distance creditable to a man of any weight and size.

I ranked next to the bottom in point of build. I weighed about a hundred and seventy pounds, and as I can best recall myself, was a rather awkward, loose-jointed performer, unskilled in thorough knowledge of athletics, a little inclined to be diffident and nervous, yet somehow, at the same time, managing to accomplish fair results without any very clear idea of how I gained them.

"Dan" Long was next above me in the matter of size. He was a magnificent specimen of a man. He stood about six feet, and weighed close to one hundred and ninety pounds. Once, I remember, in the B. A. A. club-house, he suddenly caught hold of me, pinioning my arms to my sides, and although I was in constant training, and, I think, of average strength, I might exactly as well have been a month-old baby. His muscles were iron; his strength incredibly great. I think, indeed, that a finer natural all-around athlete than Dan Long never stepped upon this earth. What he would have accomplished had he chosen to make of sport practically a profession, as so many of our "amateurs" do to-day, I can only guess. But Long, though a thorough lover of athletics, took them as recreation merely. He worked hard for his living, and much of his work had to be done at night. Under such conditions it was hardly possible for him ever to be in the very pink of physical condition; nor did he have the leisure to make of the study of athletics a fine art. To watch him at the high jump showed his method, or lack of it, to perfection. Here was none of the careful measuring of the run, the exact posturing, the almost mathematical precision of the man who has spent hours in calculating the best method of clearing the bar. Long, on the contrary, would measure the height for a moment with his eye, run blithely down at the take-off, and jump. That was all there was to it. But what a splendid jump it was — clear spring, no hitching or contortion of the body, just the natural bound of the natural jumper — and it was good for close to six feet. Whenever I think of Long's manner of performing, I am reminded of the story (which, by the way, is true) told of Peter O'Connor, the great Irish broad jumper. At the Olympic games in

Athens, in 1906, some one asked him if there was any special method to his jump. "Well," answered O'Connor, half-doubtfully, "ye see, I have a mark at so far back, and another mark beyond that. I hit the first mark easy like; then I run harder for the near one; and when I'm after hitting that, I go for all that's in me, and about four steps from the take-off I shut my eyes, and put my trust in God."

Brigham of Worcester, the fourth man of the field, was far and away the biggest of the lot. He must have weighed over two hundred pounds, but like me, he lacked experience in many of the events, and even in the weights where he should have scored most heavily, his lack of form prevented him from putting his full strength into play.

Long was really the logical winner of the event. If the four of us had stood in line, and any experienced trainer had been asked to select the best man of the four, no one, I think, could have failed to select Dan Long as the man. And yet, with all his other qualifications, he had one event in which he was woefully weak. This was the pole-vault. I do not think his failure to master the art was due to any lack of aptitude, but it was rather owing to a perfectly natural distaste (since he was a married man, with a wife and children dependent on him) for taking chances in an event which is truly dangerous to life and limb. Thus he never practised the vault, and even in competition he went at the bar gingerly, with none of the snap and dash which marked his work in the other events. And while, on the day of the all-arounds, he performed splendidly at almost everything else, and half way through the event, had a comfortable lead over the rest of the field, yet when the pole-vault was reached, he did but seven feet, while the rest of us did nearly two feet higher, and the enormous difference in points—in the neighborhood of four hundred — was too great for him to overcome. Just once, indeed, by his splendid work with the fifty-six, he temporarily regained the lead, but Carpenter in turn defeated him in the broad jump and the mile, and finally finished a winner by a hundred points, while I was another hundred behind Long.

I have called the competition a noteworthy one in some respects. And this is perfectly true. In the first place, it was remarkable as a contest; I cannot recall another all-around where three men finished such a slight distance apart, and where the winner was actually in doubt until the very last event of all. In the second place, and much more remarkable, was the good scoring. Carpenter made 5850 points; Long 5756; I made 5645, and Brigham 5409. I can recall very few all-arounds, sectional or national, where four competitors made such even scores of such high average quality.

Some of the individual performances, too, were remarkably good. Carpenter's 37 feet and 11 inches in the shot was first-class for an all-around competition; Long and I tied at 5 feet $7\frac{3}{4}$ in the high jump; Long threw 116 feet 10 with the hammer, and 27 feet 11 with the fifty-six. But the two best showings were in the broad jump and the mile. Carpenter cleared 21 feet $10\frac{1}{2}$ inches in the broad jump, I was an inch and a half behind, and Long did 20 feet and 7 inches. This was close to championship work, and was done, it must always be remembered, after eight other events, including the half-mile walk. Brigham ran the mile in 5 minutes, $9\frac{2}{5}$ seconds, and I believe I am correct in saying that no other man, in an all-around competition, ever ran such a mile, before or since. And considering Brigham's gigantic build, the feat seems more wonderful still. His record, I think, will stand for years to come.

A month later the national all-rounds were held in New Jersey. Carpenter and Long both went on to them, and as I could not see where I had a chance to win, I concluded to stay at home. It proved to be a fortunate decision, for the contest was wholly disappointing. It was a day of driving wind, with a steady downpour of rain. Good performances were impossible; Long quit the struggle in disgust, and Carpenter, continuing, was beaten by Cosgrave, of New York, who won with the lowest total ever recorded for first place in the all-arounds, 4406 points. The conditions can be imagined from Carpenter's score, 4078; nearly 2000 below his winning record in the New Englands. I was glad enough that I had stayed at home.

Thus ended my first experience with the all-arounds. I had been defeated, almost as a matter of course. But that did not discourage me in the slightest degree. I had never expected to win, and at least I had the consolation of knowing that I had been beaten by athletes of vastly greater experience than myself. I had gained, moreover, much valuable knowledge. I had been, as it were, under fire; had gone through the long programme without fatigue; and if, with the exception of the broad jump, there was nothing of real brilliance about my performances, still on the other hand there was nothing, with the possible exception of the mile, which could be called really bad. And so, with a good heart, I made up my mind to strengthen the weak places, and to try again another year.

CHAPTER VI

THROUGH the summer and autumn of 1895 the papers, from time to time, would speak of the project, then on foot, for a revival of the Olympic games, at Athens, in the spring of the following year. And yet, rather curiously as it seems to us now, in view of the excessive excitement of recent years, there was little interest in America over the plan, and it was not until the winter of 1896 that the B. A. A. decided to send a team to the games.

The whole idea sprang from a chance remark uttered in jest. At the club's annual games in January, Arthur Blake, our best distance-runner, won the thousand yards, after a spectacular finish and in very good time. After the race Mr. Burnham, one of Blake's friends and a prominent member of the club, was congratulating him on his showing, and Blake laughingly answered: "Oh, I'm too good for Boston. I ought to go over and run the Marathon, at Athens, in the Olympic games."

Mr. Burnham looked at him for a moment in silence, and then: "Would you really go if you had the chance?" he asked.

"*Would* I," Blake returned, with emphasis; and from that moment Mr. Burnham made up his mind, if it could be brought about, that the B. A. A. should send a team to the games.

A month later everything was definitely decided upon. The team was to consist of five men, — T. E. Burke for the hundred and four hundred metre runs; Blake for the mile and the Marathon; W. W. Hoyt for the pole-vault; T. P. Curtis for the hundred metres and the hurdles; and myself for the high and broad jumps. John Graham, the B. A. A. trainer, was to be in charge of the team. In the meantime, Princeton University had decided to send a team of four men, — Garrett, Tyler, Lane, and Jamison, — and James B. Connolly, now widely known as a writer of Gloucester fishing stories, took the trip upon his own account, representing the Suffolk Athletic Club, and traveling in company with the team from the B. A. A.

There remained for me one obstacle to be overcome. The others were their own masters, but I was still in college — this was in my senior year — and my going was wholly dependent upon the consent of the authorities. I went to see Dean Briggs at once, and pleaded my cause with what eloquence I possessed. He was pleasant and fair about the whole matter, telling me that he realized what an opportunity it was, and that he would like nothing better than to grant me permission; but that on the other hand, it was a long trip; that it would necessitate a break in all my college work; and that, upon the whole, he thought that he had better take my case under advisement, and give me a decision as soon as possible. Half-hoping, half-fearing, I left him. Two or three days later I entered my room to find his letter awaiting me. I drew a long breath, tried to fortify my mind against disappointment, and opened the note. The first sentence was enough. "After careful deliberation I have decided to let you go to Greece." I gave a shout that could have been heard, I believe, half way to Boston. And from that day to this I have, "in my orisons," never forgotten the kindness of the Dean. It was no small thing to ask; my fate lay wholly in his hands; and his approval gave me an opportunity which could not, as things turned out, have come again in a lifetime.

On the 20th of March, with a few friends at the station to bid us farewell, we left for New York; not one of us, it is safe to say, even dreaming of the sight that same station would present some two months later upon our return. At ten o'clock the next morning we had embarked on the North German Lloyd steamship Fulda, and had fairly set sail for the unknown.

Our first thought, of course, was to keep in good condition during the voyage, and to accomplish this we at once cast about us for the best means of getting our daily exercise. The captain, after a single glance at our spiked shoes, promptly forbade their use upon his much-prized decks; yet rubber-soled gymnasium shoes did nearly as well, and every afternoon we put on our running clothes, and practised sprinting, hurdling and jumping on the lower deck. My own specialty — the high jump — was rendered particularly interesting by the pitching and rolling of the vessel. It all depended upon whether you left the deck at the moment when the vessel was bound up or down. If the former, about two feet was the limit you might attain; if the latter, there came the glorious sensation of flying through space; a world's record appeared to be surpassed with ease; and one's only fear was of overstaying one's time in the air, and landing, not on the decks again, but in the furrow of the wake astern.

The best of weather favored us; each day the air grew more balmy; the Azores were reached and passed, and on March 30th we landed at Gibraltar. So much of interest, after our days on shipboard, there was to see! The towering rock, with its loopholes; the English soldiers, with their crisp, incisive speech; the Highlanders; the Spanish troops, over across the way; the market; the white-walled houses.

Yet we had scant time, after all, "for to admire and for to see." Ours was no mere pleasure trip; our goal still lay beyond us, and to reach it in the best shape possible — that was our first thought. After the ground had ceased, a little, to rock beneath our feet, and the houses stood bolt upright, as they should, instead of reeling dizzily from side to side, we made our way out to a race-track, a little beyond the town, and there put on our spikes and did our first real work since leaving home. The hardest work, of course, fell upon Blake, who had his long grind of twenty-five miles always before him. And so, after the rest of us had done our work and taken

FORREST C. SMITHSON

our seats in luxury in our carriages for a drive around the town, Blake, to test his wind and stamina, elected to run behind. Nor did he take his pleasure sadly. From time to time, as we passed groups of small ragamuffins standing beside the road, Blake, who possessed, together with a sense of humor, histrionic ability to a marked degree, would stoop and pretend to pick coins from the dust behind the carriages, shouting delightedly the while. The small boys were easy victims; we, from the carriages, did our best to encourage the deception; and Blake, pursued by the barefooted hunt, came gloriously along in our rear, producing an effect almost equal to the real Marathon, which was yet to come.

We left the steamer at Naples, and then began a tiresome journey. Across Italy to Brindisi, thence by boat to Patras, then another long day's journey by rail — and finally, on the evening of April 5th, we caught our first glimpse of the Acropolis, and knew that our journey eastward was at an end. The next day marked the opening of the games, and tired with travel as we were, our first thought was to get quietly to the hotel and rest. Yet no such fortune as that awaited us. The streets were thronged with people. There was a brass band of many pieces welcoming us insistently, overwhelmingly. Banners — blue and gold for the B. A. A.; orange and black for Princeton — were waving above the crowd; as if by magic, a procession formed; we found ourselves engulfed, marched away, — we knew not whither, — and the quiet of the hotel became a distant dream.

It was at some building of governmental significance that we finally arrived. Our welcome was magnificent. There were speeches — cordial, we had no doubt; lengthy, we were certain. There was champagne — much of it — and until we were able to explain the reason for our abstinence, international complications threatened. Even then, I think our hosts scarcely understood. Training? What did that signify? A strange word. Come, a glass of wine, to pledge friendship. No? Very well, then, so be it. Strange people, these Americans! Yet they forgave us courteously enough; we had a welcome of the finest; and it was late indeed when at last we reached the haven of the "Angleterre."

The next morning — April 6th, the first day of the games — dawned clear and bright. We spent the morning quietly at the hotel, and shortly before noon left for the Stadium. Up to this very moment we had no slightest idea of what the games meant to Greece; we did not know whether the huge Stadium would contain a thousand spectators or ten thousand. Yet, as we drove through the city, slowly the magnitude of the whole affair began to dawn upon us. Through the streaming crowds we came to the entrance, to find every one of the sixty thousand seats in the vast enclosure occupied, and people standing in crowds on the surrounding hills. In the space within the running-track, Samara, the Greek composer, led the musicians in his majestic "Overture to the Olympic Games." And then, shortly before two o'clock, the King, accompanied by the royal family, entered the Stadium, and in a few brief words formally opened the Olympic games of 1896.

A moment later the sound of a trumpet announced the first event — the trial heats in the hundred-metres run. One by one the contestants filed out upon the track — representatives of a dozen different nations. Those of our team whose events did not fall upon the first day were seated in the Stadium with the other spectators, looking anxiously for the three Americans, Curtis, Burke, and Lane. And then, as the runners lined up for the first heat, we saw Curtis in the middle of the line, the blue and gold unicorn of the B. A. A. showing, clear and plain, upon his breast. All in a dozen seconds the pistol cracked; Curtis leaped away in the lead, held his gain, increased it, and crossed the line a winner, with plenty to spare. At the entrance of the Stadium stood a tall flag-staff on which the flag of the nation winning each event was to be hoisted, and a moment later we saw the stars and stripes flutter out upon the breeze. It was a sight to stir the blood. Forgetting that we were in a country where college and club cheering was unknown, we sprang to out feet, and our shouts rang out most lustily across the field. "B. A. A. — 'rah, 'rah, 'rah! — B. A. A. — 'rah, 'rah — 'rah! — B. A. A., 'rah — 'rah — 'rah! — Curtis!" For a moment people turned and stared at us with a certain dazed surprise, as if wondering whence we had made our escape, and then all at once they seemed to grasp the meaning of our effort. We had, by good fortune, chanced to please the popular taste, and the cheer from that moment until we left Athens was in constant demand.

All that afternoon we heard from venturesome beginners, eager to learn, tentative and dispirited "B — ah — ahs!" and when we would cheer on our own account, their efforts to join us produced a composite discord of sound such as I never heard before, and surely never expect to hear again.

In the meantime, Lane of Princeton and Burke of Boston had won their heats in the hundred metres, and the next event, the hop, step, and jump, was under way. Here there were no trials, no qualifying for the finals on another day; the whole event was run off at once, so that this was really the first Olympic championship to be decided.

James B. Connolly was the only American entry, and we watched some dozen of the other contestants make their trials — some good, some bad, some indifferent — before at length Connolly's name was called. We, of course, knew what he [could do — he held at that time and for many years afterward the American record for the two hops and a jump — and were therefore more pleased than surprised when he hit his take-off perfectly, and landed out in the pit, almost six feet beyond his nearest competitor. The Greeks were astounded, and after that jump Connolly's popularity in Athens was assured. As he walked back to the dressing-rooms, winner of the first championship, the crowd surged around him, shouting his name, and coupling it with cries of "Nikē! nikē!" Connolly had "made good," and one prize, at least, was to come back with us across the water.

Then came the trials in the four hundred metres. Burke and Jamison won their heats, while in the eight hundred metres Flack of Australia, and Lermusiaux of France, were the winners. Last of all came the discus-throw, and here Garrett of Princeton surprised every one by managing, on his last trial, to win, by the narrow margin of inches, from the best performer among the Greeks.

April 7th, the second day of the games, was a repetition of the first. Burke won the final heat of the four hundred metres, with Jamison second; Garrett won in the shot; while Curtis of America and Goulding of England won the trials in the hundred-and-ten-metre hurdle race. Flack, the Australian, won the mile by a close margin over Blake, our entry; and I won the broad jump.

My own win was about as close a thing as it

could well have been; an experience I should not care to go through again. In America, the invariable custom is for the jumper to measure off his distance, and to mark the spot where he begins to run his hardest with his sweater, athletic programme, or something else which will readily catch the eye. I myself was very dependent on this mark, and practically lost without it. In addition, the jumping path was rough, utterly unlike the closely-rolled cinders on Holmes Field, and this might well mean a difference of a foot or more in allowing for the proper run. Thus my discomfiture may be imagined when Prince George of Greece, who was superintending the event, emphatically forbade any measurements or marks. Apparently this, to the Greek mind, savored of "professionalism." We made a faint attempt to argue, were promptly suppressed, and remembering the cautions we had received at home, lest possible international bad feeling should arise out of the games, we meekly bowed to "the umpire's decision," and proceeded to "play ball."

Connolly and Garrett both got in fair jumps, but when my turn came, I hit the take-off wrong, stepped over the board, and of course had the pleasure of hearing my jump condemned as a foul. On my second trial, I figured as closely as I could, tried to reason where I had missed it before — and fouled again. It was little short of agony. I shall never forget my feelings as I stood at the end of the path for my third — and last — try. Five thousand miles, I reflected, I had come; and was it to end in this? Three fouls, and then five thousand miles back again, with that for my memory of the games. I figured once more, got into my stride as well as I could, jumped — and won. But, as the Rogers Brothers were wont to observe, "My, what a closeness!" There were a few moments before that third trial which I have no wish to repeat.

On April 8th and 9th the gymnastic contests were held, and in these the Greeks and Germans showed to the best advantage. The only athletic event on the 9th was the final of the eight hundred metres, where Flack was an easy winner.

Friday, April 10th, was the last day of the games, and the one beside which the others sank into insignificance. The programme included the final heat of the hundred-metre run, the hurdle race, the pole-vault, the high jump,

THOMAS E. BURKE

and, by far the most important to the general public, the Marathon. The Greeks seemed to feel that the national honor was at stake; the excitement was so great as to be almost painful; and on all sides we heard the cry, "The other events to the Americans; the Marathon to a Greek."

The sight in the Stadium was one never to be forgotten. Hours before the games began, every seat was taken; the aisles, and the space between the lowest tier of seats and the running-track, were filled with people; the surrounding hills, as on the days preceding, were blackened with a dense throng; and in addition, from the entrance of the Stadium, as far as the eye could see, people stood, three and four deep, lining both sides of the road, eager to catch the first glimpse, or even the first news, of the Marathon runners, who were to start on their long journey at noon. Altogether, at least one hundred and fifty thousand people must have been present on the great final day.

The events in the Stadium were quickly decided. Burke won the final of the hundred metres; in the hurdles Curtis defeated Goulding by inches, in the most exciting finish of the games; I won the high jump; and Hoyt, after a hard tussle with Tyler of Princeton, won the vault. He had his bad quarter of a minute, as I had had mine in the broad jump. With the bar up around ten feet, Tyler got over in safety, and Hoyt missed twice. I can remember now the anxiety with which I saw him come running down the path on his last trial. His nerve held; he caught things right, and was over in safety, eventually to prove the winner.

The name of the last champion was announced; and then, suddenly, there fell utter silence over the Stadium. The same thought rose in every mind: "Who wins the Marathon?" Slowly the moments dragged, and then, on a sudden, a murmur arose in the long line of watchers outside the entrance, — a murmur which grew to a shout, and then swelled to a vast roar, — "A Greek! A Greek wins!" and a moment later, panting, dusty, travel-stained, but still running true and strong, Spiridon Loues, a young Greek peasant, burst into the Stadium, the winner of the race, the hero of the day, and the idol of his people. For a few moments the wildest confusion reigned. Snow-white doves, decked with ribbons of blue and white — the national colors — were set free in the enclosure; flowers, money, jewelry, were showered upon the victor; and completing the circuit of the track, with the Crown Prince and Prince George on either side, Loues was borne away to the dressing-rooms on the shoulders of the crowd. The second and third places were also won by Greeks, and the fourth by a Hungarian.

The after history of the race was most interesting. Lermusiaux, the Frenchman, started out at a terrific pace, and at ten miles was far in the lead, with Flack second, and Blake third. Then the Frenchman's strength failed him, and he had to stop. Blake, running strongly and easily up to fifteen miles, at that point suddenly collapsed, and fell, unable to continue. A few miles farther on, Flack followed suit, and then the Greeks, who had wisely set a slower pace, came to the front, and fought it out for the first three places among themselves.

Thus the games came to an end; yet the interest of the trip was still to continue. On the 11th we watched the bicycle races and the swimming, and in the evening were given a reception by Admiral Selfridge, on the San Francisco, then lying off the city, in the Piræus. I have the "Programme of Music" by me as I write. "The Washington Post"; "Tommy

Atkins"; "The Bowery"; eloquent reminders of the swift passage of the years.

For the next few days one event after another crowded upon us. Breakfast at the palace with the King, a ball, a picnic with the royal family, on the day when the prizes — cups, medals, diplomas, twigs of wild olive — were presented at the Stadium; it was all a time to be remembered. Other Olympic games held later were to attract greater numbers of athletes, were to result in the making of more remarkable records, but for the *time* itself, nothing could equal this first revival. The flavor of the Athenian soil — the feeling of helping to bridge the gap between the old and the new — the indefinable poetic charm of knowing one's self thus linked with the past, a successor to the great heroic figures of olden times — the splendid sportsmanship of the whole affair — there is but one first time in everything, and that first time was gloriously, and in a manner ever to be remembered, the privilege of the American team of 1896.

And still there was something more in store for us — our welcome home. None of us realized the interest which the games had awakened in our native city, and to be met in New

York by special cars, bearing our august city fathers, come to welcome us, and armed to kill two birds with one stone — it was sublime! The railroad station thronged with a surging crowd. Banquets at the B. A. A., and under the auspices of the city, in the presence of the governor and the mayor, a public reception in old Faneuil Hall, — verily wonder succeeded to wonder, and it was almost with the feeling that we had been living in a land of shadowy romance, that we settled down again to the quiet routine of every day. The Olympic games of 1896 had come and gone, leaving in our hearts an enduring memory.

CHAPTER VII

FOR some time after my return from the Athenian games I could not seem to regain my form. The New England all-arounds were held on June 17, 1896, but they were a tame affair. Neither Carpenter nor Long competed, and Brigham I never heard of again; something I have always regretted, for it seemed to me that he had the makings of a good all-around man. With all these withdrawals, only two men actually competed in the games, — E. L. Hopkins of South Boston and myself. Hopkins was a fair performer with the weights, and could walk a good half-mile, but otherwise was not particularly dangerous. This, indeed, was fortunate for me, for I was in poor form, not nearly so good even as the year before. I did a trifle better with the weights, but fell off in the other events. In fact, the only performance at all approaching merit was a broad jump of 21 feet $2\frac{1}{4}$. I went abroad again in June, and the national championship for that year was won by L. P. Sheldon of Yale. There were only three competitors and Sheldon won with 5380 points.

1897 was destined to be my banner year, in which I was to improve steadily until, in the very pink of condition, I was to meet with an injury that was to end my track career for five years. All through the spring of 1897 I was in good shape, and as soon as the intercollegiate games were ended began my training for the New England all-arounds. This year's contest was to be a very different thing from the fiasco of the year before. There were four contestants: W. J. Holland, afterwards the intercollegiate champion at the quarter-mile, W. B. Boyce of the Brookline High School, an athlete of exceptional promise, David Hennan, the Harvard weight-thrower, and myself. This year there was an innovation which really robs the contest of its value as an all-around performance. This was the substitution of the discus-throw for the half-mile walk. While we did not score as many points as we should have done at the walk, there could be no comparison, in the matter of physical exhaustion, between the taking of three throws with the discus and the terrific grind of the half-mile. But, apart from this, my performance was a very fair one. The hundred yards was a good beginning. Holland was an excellent sprinter, and won in the good time of 10⅖ seconds, but Boyce and I were only two and a half feet behind him. This was the best hundred I had ever run, and like the golfer who does his first hole in a three, it gave me good courage for the rest of the events. After that, I did a well-balanced performance: 38 feet 2¾ inches in the shot; 5 feet 8 in the high jump; 92 feet 8 with the discus; 120 feet 5¼ with the hammer; 9 feet 2¼ in the vault; 17⅛ seconds in the hurdles; 26 feet 4 with the fifty-six; 21 feet 4¼ in the broad; and, having the competition well in hand, something over 6 minutes for the mile — a total of nearly 6400 points.

Encouraged by my performance I decided to enter the national all-around championship on the Fourth of July. It so happened that the event this year attracted an unusually large number of starters. There were nine of us altogether: six New Yorkers, — Reuss, White, Mahoney, Winship, Smith, and Bloss, — Cosgrave of the New Jersey Athletic Club, Dole from California, and myself from Boston.

The day was one of terrific heat — the thermometer, as I remember, stood at 96 degrees in the shade, — and I am confident that had it not been for the good judgment of my trainer, John Graham, I should scarcely have come through the contest in as good shape as I did. My besetting sin, at that time, was a craze to do too much work. To stay out an entire afternoon in the broiling sun, diverting myself with such airy trifles as the fifty-six-pound weight, the hammer, and the half-mile walk, appeared to me a normal day's exercise. Finally, a week before the games, Graham gave me a long and serious talk, and laid down the law in language which I could not mistake. He told me that I had been through one hard all-around, and had another coming; that I had a bad ankle which needed the best of care; that I was in imminent danger of going stale; and that I was forthwith to give up all work, and rest for a week, whereby I would step onto the track on the Fourth in the best shape of my life.

I argued against him in vain, protesting that I was short of work as it was; that to lay off for a week would put me in such bad condition that I should not be able to do anything at all; and advancing many another flimsy pretext that I cannot now remember. All in vain: he was firm, and with much grumbling, I finally consented to do as he desired.

All that week I worried, devouring every jotting concerning the games which appeared in the papers; imagining myself getting so fat and out of shape that I should be unable even to run the hundred yards, and going through all the other alarms which attack a comparative novice before his first big competition. All the way on to New York I kept telling Graham what poor condition I was in, but he failed to sympathize with me in the least, telling me to do the best I could, and not to worry. Up to the very last moment before I stepped out on the track, I was in a state of pitiable nervousness. I had not lost my "nerve" as the expression goes; I felt that I was going to do every bit that was in me, but I feared that that amounted to extremely little. My heart seemed to take up the whole of my body with its pounding; my tongue was parched, my mouth dry. The talk around the grounds was that a New York man was going to win, and while in my heart I felt sure that Cosgrave was to be my chief opponent, I attributed all sorts of wonderful powers to the others, and felt myself very small indeed; so that, when the call finally came for the hundred yards, I walked over to the start, with the feeling that as far as winning went, I might exactly as well have stayed at home.

A moment later, our names were called off, and I found that I was drawn in the same heat with E. B. Bloss. I was glad of this, for while I knew he could beat me, I knew also that the stress of trying to keep up with him would probably make me run faster than if I had been drawn in a heat where I might have won, but finding myself in the lead, would insensibly have relaxed my efforts. I could not help thinking, as I watched Bloss taking a practice start down the track, that he must be far and away the smallest man who ever competed in an all-around. I speak only from memory, but I do not suppose that he was over five feet five at the most. Yet he was muscled like a giant, and as full of sheer, downright, nervous energy as any man who ever wore a shoe. "The Pocket Hercules," my friend and classmate, W. E. Putnam, Jr., the high jumper, used to call him, and the phrase was a most happy one. His records for the short dashes still stand; he was a twenty-three-foot man at the broad jump; and a good high jumper as well; but the idea of his handling a hammer or a fifty-six-pound weight was absolutely ludicrous. I shook my head as I watched him, and then stepped out on the track, to get my own muscles running smoothly, though as a matter of fact the day was so warm that the phrase "warming-up" was irony. I dug the holes for my start, crouched on the mark, and then sprang away into my stride.

Never, so long as I live, shall I forget the feeling of that moment. On the instant I knew that Graham had handled me to perfection; I had spring and bound enough in me to make me feel that I could do anything, and with a little sigh of satisfaction I sat down under the trees, and awaited the call for the first heat. Soon enough it came, and I ran the best hundred of my life. Bloss won, of course, and made the good time of $10\frac{2}{5}$; but I pressed him hard all the way, and was at his shoulder when we crossed the tape. Two feet back was the official rating, and more than satisfied, I ran across the field to change my shoes for the shot-put. Here I was to open up my first lead of consequence, for I put 37 feet $11\frac{1}{2}$ inches, while the next best was by White, who put 35, the others ranging all the way down to 30. The high jump I had all along conceded to Cosgrave, for he had a record of over 6 feet, while 5 feet 10 was my best. Evidently, however, the hard work in preparation for the other events had taken the edge off Cosgrave's jumping, for 5 feet 8½ was his limit, while I went up to 5 feet 9½ without a miss, and stopped without trying farther. After this, I had no great fear of the result, and while I walked a very poor half-mile, I made a fair throw with the hammer, 117 feet 7 inches; did 9 feet 6 in the pole-vault, and ran the hurdles in 17⅕ seconds. After this, I began to tire slightly, and made a poor throw with the fifty-six — only 23 feet and 4 inches. I broad-jumped 21 feet, and ran a slow mile, more for the sake of breaking the record than for anything else. Cosgrave was second, while Dole of California came with a rush toward the end, and finished third. His vault of 10 feet and 9 inches was the best individual performance of the day.

And now, once fairly in good form, and with a pleasant future ahead of me in the athletic world, I was destined to meet with an accident which was to cripple me for the rest of my days. In September of this same year I was on a shooting trip in Prince Edward Island. An athletic meeting was held in Charlottetown, and I was asked to give an exhibition in the high jump. The sports were held in an open field, and there was no place prepared for landing; I had a knee which had been troubling me a little, but foolishly enough I went ahead, and jumped. I had only cleared two or three low heights — the bar, I think, was around 5 feet 4 inches — when, on my next trial, I took off a little too far from the bar, gave a throw of the body to get myself over, lost my balance, and as I landed, my spikes caught in the grass, and held my leg firmly, while the rest of my body kept on. Across the track, in the grand stand, the spectators heard a report like a pistol. I turned faint and sick for a moment, and when I tried to get up on my feet, my left knee was useless. It was not broken, — the doctor told me later that a break would have been preferable, — but of the muscles and sinews and ligaments that could be torn and damaged, not one was left intact. To make it worse, I undervalued the injury, tried to walk round on the knee, and was soon in a fever, with a severe inflammation. For six weeks after I reached home, I was flat on my back, and for two years I had no thought of athletics, and was glad enough to get around about my ordinary business again.

By the spring of 1900, the knee was better, and I felt the old desire to try athletics again come back to me. E. C. White had won the title in 1898, with the very low total of 5243 points. In 1899 J. Fred Powers of Worcester won, with the excellent total of 6203 points. Powers was a remarkable athlete. At Notre Dame he was known by the nickname of "Track-Team" Powers, and indeed, it was not far from the truth. I believe he could have competed, practically single-handed, against many a team of the smaller colleges, and won his way to victory. Over 40 feet with the shot, 5 feet 11 in the high, and 21 feet $8\frac{1}{2}$ in the broad, were the pick of his records.

If Powers had announced himself as a competitor in the following year, I should not have tried the games again; for while he had not quite equaled my record of 1897, still I realized that I was in no such condition as I had been then, and could not have come within many hundred points of my old record. As it chanced, however, Powers turned professional. I forwarded my entry, and learned that there were only three others competing, — Reuss and White of New York, and a third man whose name was then unknown to the athletic world at large, Harry Gill of Canada. To me it seemed like an easy chance to score a victory, and although my knee was still bothering me, and I was generally in pretty poor shape, I had just enough foolish conceit to think that I could win, even with things as they were.

To enter a contest possessed with over-confidence is, as a general rule, to invite disaster. The trip to New York rather increased my belief that I could win. I made the journey to Bergen Point in company with some New Yorkers who had seen the games in 1897, and while I told them I was not in shape, they expressed no doubts as to the result. They did not rate Reuss and White very highly, and Gill they had never heard of.

I shall never forget the first glimpse I had of Gill, as he was stripping in the club-house. I was judge enough of athletes by this time to feel a sinking sensation as I gazed at him. And in truth he was an awkward-looking customer for any one to undertake to handle. He was about six feet tall, must have weighed, at that time, in the neighborhood of a hundred and eighty-five pounds, and was as erect and rugged as a pine tree. He was quiet and modest, had little to say for himself, but a casual practice put with the shot, before we walked over to the hundred, did not decrease my feeling that I was confronted with an exceptionally good man.

In the hundred he showed poorly; his time was 11⅖, and I had no difficulty in disposing of him. Momentarily I felt that I had overrated him, but alas, the shot-put was to disillusion me. He seemed to put so easily, and with such a lack of strain and effort, that I felt almost a sense of personal injury to see how far his puts landed beyond my own. 41 feet 5½ inches — it was a revelation. Perhaps, I thought, he will show a reversal of form in the high jump. But heavens! — when it came to the high jump, it was a case of "born and bred in a briar-patch." The same deceptive ease. He cleared the low heights with what looked like a lack of form, going over them by perhaps an inch or two. Good enough, I thought, he'll soon fail; I'll have a chance yet. But, to my amazement, he kept on clearing height after height like a machine, always with the same comfortable margin to spare. Eventually he cleared 5 feet 11½ — if memory serves me — without ever missing a height at all. It was enough; I knew when I was defeated, and for the remainder of the contest I was little more than an interested spectator. Gill, to be sure, did not keep up this tremendous pace. The shot and the high jump were the two brilliant spots in the record, but the rest of the programme was even and well-balanced. The fifty-six was especially good, 27 feet 7½; and he broke my record with a total of 6360½ points. Later he turned professional, as Powers had done, and curiously enough, these two winners of the amateur championship were to meet as professionals, in 1903, when the professional all-around championship was held at South Boston, Gill proving the winner.

After the disastrous experience of 1900, I was content to let two years go by without so much as a thought of the all-arounds. The championship in 1901, and again in 1902, went to Adam Gunn, of Buffalo, a really first-class performer, and one of the six or eight all-around champions who have merited the name. His performance in 1902 was especially noteworthy; thoroughly well-balanced, without a weak point on the list, and with a showing of 39 feet and 7 inches in the shot, and 10 feet 6, in the pole-vault. His total in points was 6260.

In the spring of 1903 I began once again to do a little work in athletics, and soon found that my knee was much stronger, and that my performances were very much better than they had been three years earlier. Continued training brought with it really encouraging results, so that by summer I made up my mind to go on to New York and take another try at the title. There were eight contestants that year, Gunn being of course the most prominent. The general feeling so far as I was concerned was, I think, one of sympathy. My last appearance had convinced every one that my day had passed, while Gunn's showing of the year before had rightly enough made him a strong favorite over the field. Up to the fifth event, the hammer-throw, it was as close a thing between us as any one could have wished to see. I won the hundred; Gunn the shot; we tied in the high jump; and I won the half-mile walk. In the hammer-throw, however, I made a trial of 122 feet and over, while Gunn had the misfortune to foul on his best throw, and scored less than 100 feet. This practically settled the contest, and I eventually won with 6318 points, just short of Gill's record in 1900. I failed by one of those close margins that I have always regretted, making a throw of about 29 feet with the fifty-six, and just putting one spike outside the circle in my effort. The difference of a half inch would have given me the record by a comfortable margin. As it was, however, I had no right to complain. My performance, like Gunn's of the year before, was a well-balanced one. I ran the hundred in 10⅘; put the shot 36 feet 7¾ inches; high-jumped 5 feet 4; threw the hammer 122 feet 8¼ inches; ran the hurdles in 17⅘; pole-vaulted 9 feet 1½; broad-jumped 20 feet 6½ ; threw the fifty-six 25 feet 5½ inches ; and ran the mile in 5.57. Altogether, I had redeemed myself for 1900.

The next year saw a new champion, in the person of T. F. Kiely of Ireland. The games were held in St. Louis, in connection with the Exposition there. Gunn competed again; so did Truxton Hare, the famous football player and hammer-thrower from the University of Pennsylvania. I was in very poor shape that spring, was half sick with bronchitis when I started for the games, and would have done infinitely better to remain at home. For the day itself was the worst on which I ever competed. It was hot and sultry, until we had reached the high jump, and then a huge black cloud bore down upon us, and in a twinkling we were caught in the hardest shower I ever saw. We were all thoroughly drenched before we could reach cover, and then stood waiting for an hour or more before we could continue. I shall never forget the high-jump path. It was a sea of mud, and between every two jumps, we must sit down with pieces of board, and scrape the mud from our jumping shoes, so that we would not slip and lose our footing altogether. When we were called to the scratch for the half-mile walk, I was in terrible condition, deathly pale, and trembling from head to foot. Yet foolishly enough, I tried to stick it out, and that walk took more out of me than anything else I ever did before or since. At its conclusion, fever succeeded to my chilliness, I made one half-hearted attempt at the hammer, and then could absolutely do no more. I was "done," and I knew it; came home with a raging fever, and was no good for the rest of the summer. So much for competing when not in shape.

It looked like a victory for Gunn until near the end, when Kiely's good work with the fifty-six helped him out, and he won, with Gunn second and Hare third. Two years later, Kiely repeated his victory, and made a score of 6274 points, giving him rank as a really first-class man. His work was the more remarkable because at this time he was no longer a young man. His performance was curious in one respect, insomuch as it was scarcely so well-balanced as with most of the really good men. His stronghold was in the weights. He was a fair performer with the shot — good for 37 or 38 feet — but with the hammer and fifty-six he scored tremendously — throwing the hammer 144 feet and some inches, and the fifty-six 31 feet 9, and just fouling on a throw of 33 feet flat. The rest of his work was hardly more than fair. He was a slow sprinter, a poor mile-runner, but a good walker. His high-jumping and pole-vaulting were weak, and his broad-jumping only fair; and yet, as I say, his hammer and fifty-six were so remarkably good that his total score ranked among the really good performances at the event.

The all-arounds of the next year, 1905, were, I think, the most successful ever held. The contest, until half the events were over, was as close as possible; the scoring was excellent; and most important of all, the games brought into prominence the foremost all-around athlete of the age — Martin Sheridan, of the Irish American Athletic Association, of New York.

There were six starters, of whom two were

hardly to be seriously reckoned with. The other four were Sheridan, Adam Gunn and Hall of Buffalo, and myself. The day was perfect, and all the conditions were favorable. I had a strong idea, from what I had heard of Sheridan's work, and from what I knew of his ability, that he would prove the winner, and I was not mistaken in my surmise. For the first five events, however, it was as pretty a contest as any one could wish. I won the hundred; Sheridan the shot; Sheridan and Gunn tied in the high jump; I won the walk, and then, in the hammer-throw, I got in a trial of 130 feet and 5 inches, to Sheridan's 112, which put me in the lead, with Sheridan a close second, and Gunn only a couple of hundred points behind.

At this point, then, I felt that unless Sheridan proved very much my superior in the pole-vault, which was the next event, I had a possible chance to win. I had never seen him vault, and knew nothing of what he could do. With the bar at about eight feet, he came out to take his first try, and as long as I live, the impression of that vault will remain on my mind. Sheridan used a pole that was immensely long; he started a long distance away from the standards, and came running down with long and powerful strides; but the distance by which he cleared the bar was the longest thing of all. I do not suppose, looking back upon it from the present time, that he really cleared the bar by six feet, but at the moment, I would have sworn to it upon the Bible. It was enough for me — I knew when I was beaten.

Not, of course, that I gave up the fight in the sense in which a man is said to "quit." But the idea which some people have that a man is capable of accomplishing wonders when threatened with defeat, is terribly overdone, and is, I believe, largely a product of school and college journalism, where the hero of the tale perceives the heroine seated in the grand-stand, and forthwith, aided by Love's heroic inspiration, wins the mile run for "dear old" Harvard or Yale or Princeton, as the case may be, incidentally shattering a world's record in the process, and that evening, at the ball, "pale and interesting-looking," is honored with the heroine's hand, and presented by her billionaire father with a brown stone front on the Avenue. This is all very beautiful. If it is a dream dear to youth, I would not seek to shatter it, merely observing that in real life, though the desire to win to please the young lady in the grand-

MARTIN J. SHERIDAN

stand, and to bring honor to one's university, are both excellent things, it is after all the weeks and months of patient preparation which are apt to tell the story; and in the common run of cases, the sudden desire, however praiseworthy, to become a hero, if it be not backed up by the careful and persistent effort to "get in shape," is apt, like a death-bed repentance, to come a little late. In a word, athletics are more a matter of mathematics, and less a matter of inspiration, than most people are wont to believe.

And thus, although I kept on vaulting to the best of my ability (which is not saying much), and although I finally cleared the greatest height I had made that year, Sheridan beat me by more than a foot, and was after that never headed, and won easily with the record score of 6820½ points. I finished second, with 6189, and Gunn third, with 6111.

Sheridan, in the matter of scoring, did not stop here. In 1907 he made a record of 7130½, and in 1909 again eclipsed his own performance with the phenomenal total of 7385.

In this last record there is scarcely a fault to be found. There are no weak points, such as might be found in Sheridan's earlier scores; by painstaking effort in his practice for the contest, he has eliminated them all, until the practically perfect score remains. $10\frac{2}{5}$ for the hundred; 43 feet $1\frac{1}{4}$ in the shot; 5 feet 7 in the high; 3.43 for the walk; 125 feet 10 in the hammer; 10 feet 9 in the pole; $17\frac{1}{5}$ in the hurdles; 20 feet $7\frac{1}{2}$ in the broad; 29 feet $11\frac{1}{2}$ with the fifty-six; and 6.05 in the mile; he must indeed be a captious critic who will venture to suggest an improvement upon this as a piece of all-around work.

Thus Sheridan stands alone among the great all-around men. No other athlete has ever reached seven thousand points; I believe it will be many years before Sheridan finds himself troubled with overmuch company.[1]

In the next rank, Gill and myself are the only men who have exceeded sixty-three hundred points. Powers, Gunn, and Kiely have made sixty-two hundred; Jordan made over sixty-one hundred. It is a hard contest; there is no gainsaying it; and the man who reaches six thousand points has a right to declare that he knows, at least, a little something about all-around work.

[1] Since this chapter was written, the all-arounds of 1910 have produced two first-class men, in F. C. Thompson of Los Angeles and J. H. Gillis of Vancouver. Thompson scored 7009 points, and Gillis 6927.

CHAPTER VIII

NEXT after the spring of 1896, when we made our trip to Greece, I think the autumn of 1895 was the most memorable period of my athletic career. Not that my performances were as good as they were two years later, for they fell short of them by a very considerable margin; but it was a time when two years of good hard practising in four or five events at once was just beginning to show results, so that I was able, in consequence, in the course of two or three months, thoroughly to satisfy my appetite for the spoils of conquest, and to see at the same time most of the great athletes of a great athletic year.

I began my campaign in July, at the meeting of the St. Mary's Athletic Association, in Boston. I won the high jump, the fifty-six-pound weight, and the three standing jumps, — breaking the B. A. A. record in the last event, — and was second in the shot. Early in September I took part in the members' games of the Newton Athletic Association, won three firsts, and established three records for the Club — 5 feet 9½ in the high; 21 feet 7¼ in the broad, and 37 feet 1½ in the shot.

Next after this, I chanced to hear of the championships of the Maritime Provinces, and nothing would do but that I should board a train, bound in a general northerly direction, and go voyaging up to Moncton, New Brunswick, to see what the Provinces were like. It was a delightful trip. Never in my life have I fallen in with people kinder or more hospitable, and I enjoyed every moment of my stay. Incidentally, I won five first prizes — the high and broad jumps, the hurdles, the shot, and the hammer, and in the high jump and the broad left new marks behind me — 5 feet 10⅝ in the high, and 21 feet 6 in the broad.

A week or so later, I went on to New York for the national championships. This was the year when the London Athletic Club sent over their team for their dual games with the New York A. C., and it was a great lot of athletes who came up from Travers Island for the games. I tried only two events, the high and broad jumps, and finished third in the high, and second in the broad. George Gray, I remember, did not compete in the shot, and Conneff stayed out of the distance runs, but with those exceptions, the New York team was practically the same as that which later faced the Englishmen. Wefers won the hundred in $9\frac{4}{5}$, and the two-twenty in $21\frac{2}{5}$, with Crum second in both events. Burke won the quarter in $49\frac{3}{5}$, and Kilpatrick the half in 1.56.2. Orton won the mile and Bean the three miles. In the high jump, Sweeney won, as a matter of course; Hickok took the shot, and Mitchell the hammer and fifty-six, throwing 139 feet $3\frac{1}{2}$ with the hammer, and 32 feet $7\frac{1}{2}$ with the weight. "Steve" Chase won the hurdles, in $15\frac{3}{5}$, and Bloss took the broad jump, with 22 feet 2.

A week later came the internationals, a complete and sweeping victory for America. Every first place went to the home team. Wefers won the hundred in $9\frac{4}{5}$, with Bradley of England second, and Crum third; and repeated his victory in the two-twenty, winning in $21\frac{3}{5}$, with Crum second. The quarter was the most exciting race of the day, Burke winning, almost in the last stride, over Jordan and Fitzherbert, the two Englishmen, in 49 seconds flat. In the half, Kilpatrick ran his greatest race, winning over Horan of England, in 1.53.2, the first quarter being run in a fraction over 54 seconds. Conneff won the mile, with Orton second, in 4.18.1, and later won the three miles in 15.36.3. Chase won over Godfrey Shaw, the English champion, in the high hurdles, in $15\frac{2}{5}$.

In the field, America's victories were even more decisive. Mitchell won the hammer, with 137 feet $5\frac{1}{2}$, and Gray the shot, with 43 feet 5. Bloss cleared 22 feet 6 in the broad jump, and in the high, Sweeney performed the feat which will live forever in athletic history, making his world's record of 6 feet $5\frac{5}{8}$ inches.

The following week, I made another of my "little journeys." The New York A. C. held their fall games at Travers Island, and it occurred to me that it would be a pleasant way of spending a Saturday afternoon to go on to them. I have never regretted that trip. Travers Island is a perfect spot under almost any conditions, but that day it was at its finest. A warm, bright autumn afternoon; a splendid crowd to witness the sports; a band that could play popular music in a fashion truly magical — I fairly radiated energy as I sat waiting for the first event to be called. That band, and its leader — they stand out with the utmost distinctness in my mind. It was the hour of the tuneful and pleasing melody, "The Band Played On." Half a dozen times in the course of the afternoon, they repeated it, always ending amid a very roar of applause. The leader — Heaven bless him! — would turn, bow and smile, rap with his baton, and once more his musicians would crash forth the verse, come to those three witching, delightful notes which marked the transition from song to chorus, and then once again, "*Casey* would dance with the strawberry blonde," and the band, in very truth, "played on." I recall music and musicians with a sigh for times departed. "The good old times"; it is always the same story; we do not have meetings like that now.

And what a field was there! My first event, I remember, was the broad jump, and I can recall most vividly seeing W. B. Rogers take his first try at the event. He was an athlete of rare ability, — a year later he was to become national champion at the high hurdles, — and possessed, when in his best shape, a tremendous amount of spring. He was allowed that day a handicap of 3 inches, which was quite unnecessary. He came tearing down across the field, shot up into the air in a manner which made me gasp, and landed away out across the pit, almost to the farther edge. It was a beautiful leap — 23 feet, and $\frac{1}{2}$ inch — and Rogers did not have to worry further about the ownership of the prize. It was his without his handicap.

Then came the hammer. I had a handicap of 25 feet over "Jim" Mitchell, and felt that if I could equal my practice work, I had a very fair chance to win. Yet somehow, in my eagerness to get in a good throw, I fouled on both of my first two attempts, and began to despair. And then, in the interval between the second and third rounds, Hickok of Yale stepped up to me, and good-naturedly told me that if I would alter the position of my left foot a little, I would have no trouble in staying in the ring. I thanked him most gratefully, followed his advice, and on my last trial got in a fair throw of 117 feet, and heard myself, a few moments later, announced as the winner. Pleased? No need to answer that question. And grateful to Hickok for that chance piece of kindly advice? No need to ask that, either. I suppose he never thought of it again, but it has stayed in my memory from that day to this.

In the meantime, the events on the track were being run off. Stage won the fifty yards, with Bradley of England second, and Bloss .

third; Wefers won the three hundred; Burke the six hundred; and Kilpatrick the thousand. In the hurdles Chase again defeated Shaw, and in the same splendid time — 15⅗.

I continued to have good luck in the field events. I finished second in the high jump; second in the shot; and third in the hop, step. Altogether it was one of the days to be remembered with pleasure, from beginning to end.

My last two meetings of the year were the New England championships, where I won the shot, and was second in the high and broad jumps, and the Harvard Fall Meeting, where I won the high jump and the hammer-throw, breaking the Harvard record in the latter event, and was second in the broad jump and the shot.

Thus I had competed in seven meetings, three of them championships, and had won twenty-eight prizes. My desire to see something of outside competition was satisfied, and I never again went "campaigning" in so thorough and business-like a manner. Yet I enjoyed it all thoroughly, and the people I met, and the great performers whom I saw have left me with a recollection of that season which could not be more pleasant to look back upon.

How the long procession of champions flashes through one's mind, looking back over the races and records of thirty years! How many sterling sprinters have done their "ten, one"; their "even time"; their "nine, four"! Myers, Ford, Sherrill, Westing, Owen, Cary, Jewett, Stage, Wefers, Jarvis, Kraenzlein, Long, Sears, Walsh, Hahn, Parsons — what a sight, to have had them, each in his prime, lined up on the mark for one great "hundred"; a championship of champions, past and present; a sight to have crossed a continent to see! And, mindful of the warning against comparisons, who will pick a man to compare with Wefers in his prime — champion at the hundred and two-twenty in 1895, 1896, and 1897! the equal of the best in the shorter dash, and at the furlong, beyond all question, the greatest and most consistent performer the world has yet seen.

Verily, this team of 1895 was a great one. Look again to the past and present of the quarter. The great Myers, — six times in succession the winner of the title, — Dohm, Downs, Burke, Long, Waller, Taylor, Hillman — here again it would be hard to dethrone Burke, the rangy champion of 1895. Myers, I suppose, —

BERNARD J. WEFERS

CHARLES H. KILPATRICK

attempting the impossible by trying to allow for the difference in the conditions under which the men competed — Myers, perhaps, was a greater runner than Burke; "Maxey" Long, at the height of his career, established the fastest records yet known; and still, year in and year out, as a racer, tried and never found wanting, as a seasoned campaigner, knowing all the theory and practice of the game, it is no light task to attempt to supplant Burke at the quarter-mile. Look at his records for the three years when he was national champion — 1895, 1896, and 1897: 49⅗, 48⅘, 49 flat; I speak subject to correction, but I can recall no other quarter-miler who ran so many of his races under 50 seconds — it became, with Burke, almost a matter of habit to run somewhere down in the forties, whenever he faced the starter. A great quarter-miler, ranking with the best.

Nor is the 1895 team to be beaten in the half. Look at the list of the great half-milers: Myers, Goodwin, Dadmun, Turner, Kilpatrick, Cregan, Burke, Lightbody, Sheppard — and to come down to this very year, Gissing and Lunghi. Kilpatrick was champion in 1894, 1895, and 1896, and his times were all good — 1.55.4, 1.56.2, and 1.57.3. Yet I think time never worried Kilpatrick a great deal; he won his races, — that was the principal thing, — and he was alone in his class. When that one supreme occasion arose in 1895, and the Englishmen had to be faced, his 1.53.2 was the result. And it remained for fourteen years, until 1909 saw Lunghi's phenomenal half at the Canadian championships, in 1.52.4. "Mel" Sheppard, of course, at once suggests the nearest approach to Kilpatrick, as a champion and a consistent performer, as well. Witness his three championships in 1906, 1907, and 1908: 1.55.2, 1.55.1, 1.55.3 — great records those! Witness his double win at the Olympic games, at London, in 1908, when he established two new Olympic records; 1.52.4 for the eight hundred metres; 4.03.2 for the fifteen hundred metres. And yet, if one can say that there has been, since Kilpatrick's day, a half-miler greater than himself, which is, for a number of reasons, always an arguable point, such a contention would amount, at best, to little more than a profitless splitting of hairs.

Coming now to the mile, where, since the days of 1895, can we find another "Tommy" Conneff, with his record of 4.15.3? Fredericks, Carter, Orton, Cregan, Alec Grant, Lightbody,

Sullivan, Trube, — there have been plenty of good men on the championship list, but that record of 4.15.3, made at Travers Island in August of 1895, still hangs on in most amazing fashion. If I were to hazard a prophecy, — always a dangerous thing to do, and especially so for one who knows little of the distance game, —it would appear to me that Paull of Pennsylvania is the man who will some day set new figures for the distance. Surely his 4.17.4, at the intercollegiates of 1909, was a performance placing him at once in the very foremost rank of the champions at the mile.

In the high hurdles it is true that "Steve" Chase would no longer be invincible, as he was in 1895. Alec Jordan, Ducharme, Puffer, Copeland, — all these were great men before him, — yet no one of them was quite his equal. But with the appearance of Kraenzlein we acknowledge for the first time a superior, and the great trio which represented America at the Olympic games in London — Smithson, Garrels, and Shaw — are all, I suppose, faster men. And yet, for all that, how slight the improvement has been over such a length of time! From $15\frac{3}{5}$ in Chase's day to $15\frac{1}{5}$ in Kraenzlein's, and finally to 15 flat in the days of Forrest Smithson. If Chase must make a bow to these latter-day heroes it is no very deep one, surely; more a friendly nod of salutation to equal masters of the same craft.

In the field events improvement in fifteen years has been a little more marked than on the track; yet not so much greater after all. For first of all in the high jump no one has risen to take the place of M. F. Sweeney. That 6 feet 5⅝ still defies all attempts to displace it, and from all appearances is still safe for many years to come. Nor have I the least doubt that if Sweeney had been forced to it by some man nearly his equal he could have improved even upon that wonderful mark. He was a marvel, possessing speed, spring, and something else as well — the ability of the thorough gymnast to handle his body to perfection, every fraction of a second, from the moment he began his run until he landed in safety on the farther side of the bar. The first time I ever saw Sweeney jump was in a special match with Phil Stingel, then the New England champion. Sweeney allowed Stingel a handicap of three inches, and the Boston man proved himself no mean antagonist. Both were graceful and finished jumpers, and both took height after height, without a miss, until they had cleared six feet in safety. Then Stingel failed; Sweeney had the bar placed at 6 feet $3\frac{1}{8}$ and was over at his first attempt. And all this was in a tiny indoor gymnasium with scarcely room enough to get the proper distance for the necessary run at the bar. I jumped against Sweeney many times myself, and never have I met with a more quiet and modest champion. He never talked about his own prowess, was always interested in the work of the other men competing, and was in every way the ideal athlete and companion. The name of W. Byrd Page, with his leap of 6 feet 4, is the one great one before Sweeney's time; since his day, Baxter, Winsor, Moffitt, and Porter have all made great records at the game; but the equal of this wonderful jumper has yet to be found.

In the broad jump the name of E. B. Bloss does not stand out as conspicuously as it did in the days of the great team which we are now estimating. Not that Bloss was not a fine performer. He was, as his records and lists of championships prove. He was three times national champion, twice champion at the intercollegiates, and a twenty-three-foot man into the bargain. Before him, other great broad-jumpers were Malcolm W. Ford, five times champion, Alec Jordan, Halpin, with his winning jump of 23 feet, in 1888, Copeland and Reber, both of whom exceeded that distance, Goff, the all-around champion — good broad-jumpers have always been plenty; — and then, succeeding directly to Bloss, come the two giants at the game, Prinstein and Kraenzlein, with their astonishing records of 24 feet $7\frac{1}{4}$ and 24 feet $4\frac{1}{2}$; Dan Kelly, of Oregon, with his 23 feet 11, and last of all, the surprise of the Olympic games at London, F. C. Irons of Chicago, with his winning leap of 24 feet $6\frac{1}{2}$.

In the weights, also, the glory of Gray and Mitchell has at last been eclipsed. But what a length of time the two men remained unbeatable! Before Gray's time, Lambrecht had won the championship with the shot for six years in succession, from 1881 to 1886, inclusive. And then George Gray appeared upon the scene. Beginning in 1887, with the exception of one year, — 1895, — when he did not compete, he held the title continuously for ten years, winning for the last time in 1896; and then, after the lapse of half a dozen years, competing again in 1902, and winning with a put of 46 feet 5, only 7 inches short of his great record of

47 feet, made in 1893, and long the record for the world. Small wonder that the names of other champions do not trouble us much, after a reign of this length. A few famous names we may find from time to time — Hickok, Sheldon, Horgan of Ireland, Beck of Yale, and finally, in 1905, W. W. Coe of Boston made his famous put of 49 feet 6, which stood as the record until 1907, when Ralph Rose, the western giant, beat Coe's mark by a half inch, and in 1909, for the first time in the history of athletics, actually achieved a distance of 51 feet!

Great as Rose's fame is to-day, I am not quite sure that his powers as an athlete, excepting by those who follow the sport closely, are really appreciated to the full. It is a common occurrence to hear some one say: "Rose? Oh, yes, if I were as big as that fellow, *I* could put a shot fifty feet." Yet size — alone — is not the secret of his success. There are bigger men than Rose in the world; not a great many, I dare say, but still some. But Rose has the necessary knowledge of the game. He is not only a marvelous shot-putter, but a fine performer with the discus, the hammer, and the fifty-six. All in all, the most wonderful all-around weight man of to-day.

Even as Gray's record in the shot has been beaten, so, too, in the hammer and fifty-six, the marks made by James S. Mitchell have been eclipsed. Yet what a record Mitchell has left behind him! A champion for twenty years, — from 1885 to 1905, — with a list of victories so staggering that a volume could be devoted to them. Four times champion of Ireland with the hammer and fifty-six, three times champion of England with the hammer, nine times champion of America with the hammer, and ten times with the fifty-six, six times champion of Canada with both, and a few shot and discus championships thrown in for good measure — surely the name of James S. Mitchell is deservedly one of the greatest in all athletic history.

Before Mitchell's day W. B. Curtis, Lambrecht, Coudon, Queckberner, and Barry were the champions. With the coming of John Flanagan, first with his double, and then with his triple, turn in the hammer, and with his double turn in the fifty-six, the old records had to go. I threw against Flanagan, shortly after his arrival in this country, at the games of the old Newton Athletic Club. He did not then have his thorough mastery of the event which

RALPH ROSE

he was later to acquire; the wire hammer-handles, I remember, kept breaking, and that disturbed him; altogether, I was a bit disappointed, after all that I had heard of his performances. But I can remember how his size and build impressed me, and what a pleasant talk I had with him about athletics on both sides of the water. We had a crowd of spectators, I recall, which seemed to me quite large, and Flanagan, after asking me if it was an average attendance, good-naturedly observed that they turned out in better numbers at home, just to watch him at his daily practice. A few years later, when I competed abroad myself, I appreciated the truth of what he told me. Ten thousand people at a little two-for-a-cent set of Saturday afternoon games, — three or four thousand at the games of a little country parish, — it was all a revelation to me. Surely we may learn, in this respect, from our English friends. It is "sport for sport's sake" with them; the blight of the "world's record" has not yet fallen upon the spirit of their play.

Other first-class performers with the hammer to-day are Matt McGrath of the New York A. C., A. D. Plaw of California, and Lee J. Talbot of Cornell, yet Flanagan, as the actual performer, — the sure man in an event notoriously uncertain, — always to be depended upon in an emergency, is the leader to-day, and bids fair to remain so until he wearies of the long list of championships which now lie behind him — a modest, quiet giant, a master of his specialties, a fit successor to Mitchell as a many times champion and record-holder — both with glory undimmed, so long as athletic history shall endure.

Thus, to come back to the point whence I have rambled away, that season of 1895 was a notable one in the history of track and field, and one that I like always to recall. Yet in 1896 as well, I had some pleasant experiences. After our return from the Olympic games I won the all-around championship of New England for the first time, and later went abroad again and competed in England a number of times that summer. Apparently the climate did me no good, for my performances were poor. At home I was doing 5 feet 9 and 10, consistently, in the high jump, yet abroad 5 feet 6 meant hard work for me. But it was good fun — I made many friends, got more or less in touch with the English point of view concerning athletics, and was altogether sorry when I had to come home again. I competed four times after my return. In the national championships I won second in the high jump; in the New England championships, which I entered without preparation, I finished second in the high hurdles and hammer, and third in the high jump, shot, and mile walk; after which I took a flying trip to Canada, winning second in the high jump, shot, and high hurdles, and third in the fifty-six. I ended the season with the Fall games at Harvard, where I first began to round into form for my lucky year, — 1897, — winning five seconds — in the shot, hammer, high jump, high hurdles, and broad jump, and doing good performances in all five.

Plenty of other memories come back to me, as I glance up at my medal-case — the two national all-arounds, of 1897 and 1903; the high-jump medal of 1907, when I was caricatured in one of the New York papers as an old-timer who thought he still had a "kick" left in him, and then turned the tables by clearing 5 feet 10, in Madison Square Garden, the best actual jump of the evening, and winning first place in the event. Similarly, the New England all-around championships of 1909 and 1910, regarded in the light of "fruit from an old tree," are recent and not undervalued trophies. It seems a far cry from the tarnished five-cent piece, with its faded ribbon, — the prize of 1889, — to the gold medals of to-day — the championships of twenty years later. But I grow garrulous — the twenty years is ended — and the chapter as well.   .

POSTSCRIPT

THE giving of advice is one of those useless luxuries with which we indulge ourselves in our advancing years. If this brief afterword savors of "preaching" let the youthful athlete deride it, and acquire his experience for himself. It has one merit, — it is brief.

As regards the physical side of athletics, don't begin too young. There is plenty of time. Don't overdo. The age of the Marathon craze will pass. A young man can have no healthier taste than a liking for athletics, but he should take his exercise rationally, and stop short of exhaustion. Take care to have yourself looked over by a competent physician, and aim to make your athletics improve your health and not endanger it.

As regards the mental side of athletics, make up your mind that there is a science of each separate event, and set your wits to work to solve it. Watch good performers; study pictures of famous athletes in action; train, if possible, with men who understand their events; unconsciously you will imitate their form. Remember that perseverance and intelligent practice accomplish wonders.

As regards the moral side of athletics, play fair. You are going to do your best to win; that is natural and right. But don't regard every competitor as an obstacle in your path; look upon him as a friend, with the same interests and ambitions as your own. You cannot be everything. It is a large world. Contestants are many, and champions rare. But there is a lot of good, healthy fun to be gained from athletics, and not the least part of it is the trying to make the most of those abilities with which Nature has seen fit to furnish you. Do your *honest best* and you have done something which, in itself, is thoroughly worth while.

INDEX

INDEX